Cancer

22 June – 23 July

*First published in Great Britain 2008
by Harlequin Mills & Boon Limited,
Eton House, 18-24 Paradise Road, Richmond, Surrey TW9 1SR*

Copyright © Dadhichi Toth 2007, 2008 & 2009

ISBN: 978 0 263 86907 1

Typeset at Midland Typesetters Australia

*Harlequin Mills & Boon policy is to use papers that are
natural, renewable and recyclable products and made from
wood grown in sustainable forests. The logging and
manufacturing processes conform to the legal environmental
regulations of the country of origin.*

*Printed and bound in Spain
by Litografía Rosés S.A., Barcelona*

About
Dadhichi

Dadhichi is one of Australia's foremost astrologers, and is frequently seen on TV and in the media. He has the unique ability to draw from complex astrological theory to provide clear, easily understandable advice and insights for people who want to know what their future may hold.

In the 25 years that Dadhichi has been practising astrology, and conducting face and other esoteric readings, he has provided over 9,000 consultations. His clients include celebrities, political and diplomatic figures and media and corporate identities from all over the world.

Dadhichi's unique blend of astrology and face reading helps people fulfil their true potential. His extensive experience practising western astrology is complemented by his research into the theory and practice of eastern forms of astrology.

Dadhichi has been a guest on many Australian television shows and several of his political and worldwide forecasts have proved uncannily accurate. He has appeared on many of Australia's leading television networks and is a regular columnist for several Australian magazines.

His websites www.astrology.com.au, www.facereader.com and soulmate.com.au which attract hundreds of thousands of visitors each month, offer a wide variety of features, helpful information and services.

Dedicated to The Light of Intuition

Sri V. Krishnaswamy—mentor and friend

With thanks to Julie, Joram, Isaac and Janelle

Welcome from
Dadhichi

Dear Friend,

It's a pleasure knowing you're reading this, your astrological forecast for 2009. There's nothing more exciting than looking forward to a bright new year and considering what the stars have in store and how you might make the most of what's on offer in your life.

Apart from the anticipation of what I might predict will happen to you, of what I say about your upcoming luck and good fortune, remember that astrology is first and foremost a tool of personal growth, self-awareness and inner transformation. What 'happens to us' is truly a reflection of what we're giving out; the signals we are transmitting to our world, our universe.

The astrological adage of 'As above, so below' can also be interpreted in a slightly different way when I say 'As within, so without'! In other words, as hard as it is to believe, the world and our experiences of it, or our relationships and circumstances, good or bad, do tend to mirror our own belief systems and mental patterns.

It is for this reason that I thought I'd write a brief introductory note to remind you that the stars are pointers to your wonderful destiny and that you must work with them to realise your highest and most noble goals. The greatest marvel and secret is your own inner self! Astrology reveals these inner secrets of your character, which are the foundation of your life's true purpose.

What is about to happen to you this year is exciting, but what you *do* with this special power of knowledge, how you share your talents with others, and the way you truly enjoy each moment of your life is far more important than knowing *what* will happen. This is the key to a 'superior' kind of happiness. It will start to open up to you when you live in harmony with your true nature as shown by astrology.

I really hope you enjoy your coming twelve months, and gain new insights and fresh perspectives on your life through studying your 2009 horoscope. Here's hoping great success will be yours and health, love and happiness will follow wherever you go.

I leave you now with the words of a wise man, who once said:

Sow a thought, and you reap an act;
Sow an act, and you reap a habit;
Sow a habit, and you reap a character;
Sow a character, and you reap a destiny.
Your thoughts are the architects of your destiny.

Warm regards, and may the stars shine brightly for you in 2009!

Your Astrologer,

Dadhichi Toth

Contents

The Cancer
Identity

If you do not hope, you will not find what is beyond your hopes.

—St Clement of Alexandra

Cancer: A Snapshot

Key Characteristics

Nurturing, sensitive, receptive, flexible, sensual, loyal, intuitive, generous, over-reactive and moody

Compatible Star Signs

Taurus, Virgo, Scorpio, Capricorn, Pisces

Key Life Phrase

I nurture

Life Goals

To be happy emotionally and in family life; to be of service to others

Platinum Assets

Great intuition, adaptability and sincerity

Zodiac Totem

The Crab

Zodiac Symbol

♋

Zodiac Facts

Fourth sign of the zodiac; cardinal, fruitful, feminine, moist

Element
Water

Famous Cancers

Julius Caesar, Cyndi Lauper, Mike Tyson, Meryl Streep,
Carly Simon, George Orwell, Kevin Bacon, Tom Hanks,
John Cusack, Kathy Bates, Sylvester Stallone, Ernest Hemingway,
Liv Tyler, Pamela Anderson, Princess Diana, Jerry Hall,
Ringo Starr, Dalai Lama, George W. Bush, Harrison Ford,
Nelson Mandela, Carlos Santana

Key to karma, spirituality and emotional balance

Your past life experiences affect this current life and because Pisces is strongly connected to your previous life, it has made you who you are. Your compassionate and almost universal love for others is part of your caring character.

Your key words are 'I nurture' so your challenge in this lifetime is to balance your desire to love with your own need for warmth, love and security. Learning to receive will be just as important as learning to give.

On Mondays and on the new and full Moons, meditate and connect with your inner powers of intuition and psychic abilities. Moonstone and white colours are beneficial.

Cancer: Your profile

To be born under the sign of Cancer is truly a karmic blessing. As well as relating to your sensitive emotional nature, it represents a development spiritually as the water signs are strongly linked to the higher evolutionary processes within us.

Simply put, Cancer, you're basically a selfless, caring and loving person who likes to demonstrate love for others.

You're also very intuitive and often exhibit an uncanny ability to go to the heart of things without any intellectual claptrap.

Another great quality of yours is adaptability. Like water you can move and change to fit the circumstances and to accommodate the people you deal with. Although you have a very strong mind when it comes to your own desires and needs, you're still able to compromise when you feel it supports the group as a whole.

Being a water sign you have a cooling yet invigorating aspect to your personality. In tough times people have a tendency to be drawn to your selflessness and nurturing traits as they know your open ear and warm heart will help them through their difficult times.

The fourth sign of the zodiac, under which you were born, relates to the domestic sphere of life and therefore you love to be part of a family network. It is here that you really excel and do your best. The Cancer home is very comfortable and even strangers usually feel quite at ease when invited to spend time in your company.

Many Cancers extend this caring, nurturing vibe to their professional activities as well. It comes so easily to you that it's no wonder you're able to work in healing and consoling professions. Your key life phrase 'I nurture' demonstrates this fact. When you read the segment on the best professions suited to you, you'll see what I mean.

Your star sign is very sensitive and you effortlessly tune in to other people's vibrations, moods and thinking processes so you are able to understand others instinctively. Your perception about their character is usually spot on.

There is a downside to this, however, as you also tend to absorb the negative emotions of others in the process. If you feel this is overloading you, you need to get yourself out of the situation quickly, even for a short time, to recover your clarity and peace of mind.

Cancer and its ruler the Moon reflect much of your own personality and, because the Moon regulates the emotions, you can find yourself challenged by incredibly extreme mood swings. Even though your family and friends are well aware of this it can be a little trying for all concerned at times.

As a woman you have maternal and nurturing qualities so you'll be absolutely well suited to the roles of homemaker and mother. Men born under Cancer also fare well as caregivers and so sometimes they exchange their roles as they do such a good job of looking after the kids, too.

Be careful not to lock yourself away in your own private lifestyle because being reclusive, enjoying your own company, can sometimes overtake your desire to connect to the world at large. Don't deny others the wonderful qualities you have to offer.

Cancers are often nocturnal as the Moon shines most brightly in the evening hours. You'll feel creative and enjoy that stillness and reflective quality of the night hours.

Many Cancers take their cooking skills to a new height by starting restaurants and showing their love of the world at large through this very unique skill. Music, writing and also gardening seem to be popular pastimes for Cancers. You'll never forget a kind deed and always reciprocate tenfold. You appreciate that same caring attitude in others.

You also realise you're more nostalgic than many other star signs and memories are important to you, keeping scrapbooks and old shoeboxes full of black and white photos as mementos of the good old times.

Cancer has a wonderfully expressive and inviting face. Because the eyes are the windows to the soul, and your eyes are large and expressive, people feel as though your heart is open enough for them and you are guileless in the way you share your thoughts and feelings.

Three classes of Cancer

If you're a Cancer who was born between the 22nd of June and the 3rd of July you have an extra dose of lunar energy as part of your makeup. You are exceedingly emotional and reciprocal in the way you express yourself romantically. Marriage and family life is a wonderful life for you but you must learn to manage your emotions, which can sometimes get the better of you.

If you were born between the 4th and 13th of July your mind is much more focused than the typical Cancer and this can also lead you to be particularly intense and possessive in your relationships. You demand loyalty; to you unconditional love is the key to a satisfactory relationship. Just remember that too much possessiveness can scare others away.

As a Cancer born between the 14th and 23rd of July, your ideals are sometimes not in keeping with the reality of life. You need to become a little more practical and then your compassionate and caring nature can find a proper outlet for your success to ripen. You'll always be surrounded by friends and family and seem to always be giving to others. Don't forget to give yourself some TLC and quality time as well.

Cancer role model: Nelson Mandela

Caring for one's own family and the world at large is one of the traits exhibited by Cancer and this is epitomised by Nelson Mandela. Always sticking to his ideal of putting his fellow country people before himself, he persisted with his dream until he was released from gaol and rid his country of apartheid.

Cancer: The light side

Because you're so connected to your feelings and understand how feelings affect others, you're able to make this a part of your life, which impacts favourably on those with whom you come in touch. You're a deep ocean of sensitive knowledge and your open and generous nature puts you at the top of everyone's list of favourite people.

Your openness and warmth need to be monitored, however, as other unscrupulous people will take advantage of you. You can be shrewd and perceptive when it comes to choosing friends and this is more the case that your intuition has been developed and you're able to see into others' motivations.

Many Cancers have an incredible arsenal of general knowledge that surprises others. You probably like to read a lot and are curious about this, that and the other. Overall, your nurturing spirit is the highlight of your sign and that will always hold you in good stead, wherever you go.

Cancer: The shadow side

It's not often evident but you can be rather dark emotionally and once people see this it can adversely affect their perception of you. Along with the fact that you're sometimes stubborn, it seems you may be a complex individual to deal with.

Sometimes an innocent comment can set you off and underneath that calm exterior your emotions will be boiling over, sulking about what someone's said. You can blame this on the Moon, which tends to heighten your sensitivity to the world and people around you. Occasionally you don't take too kindly to constructive criticism, seeing it as an attack on your nature rather than an intention to do good things.

Although your sensitivity to your environment is an asset, you must be careful not to let these dramatic mood swings undermine your life and relationships.

Much of these problems relate to your early life and some Cancers need to get more in touch with this part of their nature to overcome these sometimes overwhelming feelings.

Cancer woman

Being born under Cancer and therefore being ruled by the Moon highlights the feminine aspect of your personality. Sensuality and loving are natural parts of who you are and they are obvious to anyone who has the pleasure of meeting you for the first time.

Sometimes, even though you feel withdrawn, shy and might not say much, your look and your grace say more than words. You also need time to tune in to and trust others before coming out of your shell. Remember, Cancer is ruled by the crab, which is hard on the outside and soft on the inside. Meryl Streep, who is also a Cancer, seems to exude this very same quality: demure, graceful, yet firm and decisive at the same time.

Your popularity goes hand in hand with your ability to understand others. Because you show so much interest in people they naturally open up to you and sense your unconditional love for them. You'd be surprised to find out just how many people hold you in high esteem, even though you might not be aware of it.

Cancer is usually patient and prepared to bide time to achieve ambitions that they set for themselves. These may not be worldly ambitions, either, as the Cancer woman tends to symbolise the ideal of motherhood and family life. These goals are just as valid and may be even more important than the shallow acquisition of power, wealth, pomp and circumstance.

In your assessment of others, you are an expert, even though you haven't particularly studied any psychological techniques. Trust that intuition of yours because it's very powerful and will help you in making decisions on the right people to have in your life.

Sometimes, when you ignore your inner promptings, which tell you when others are not right for you, or that their integrity is lacking, you later regret not trusting yourself. In time you'll learn that you can avoid many of the hardships in your life, simply by trusting your gut feelings.

There are quite a few different types of Cancers, from the classy Meryl Streep, whom I just mentioned, through to the wacky but lovable Cindy Lauper and world-famous Princess Diana. All have their own unique character but tend to exhibit that similar soft and lovable streak. You may be any or all of these people all wrapped in one big bundle of womanly love.

Marriage will be the highlight of your life and is a particularly important commitment, too. Even if you are progressive in many other areas, you'll be conservative and very traditional when it comes to this aspect of your chosen path. You're drawn to having a family and will slot into the role of parenthood very easily. Casual affairs and one-night stands will never feel comfortable for you. You'll be constantly seeking the love of your life that can fulfil this very deep and important need.

You especially love to dote on children, lavishing your love and warmth upon them with demonstrative action. Rearing children will be a very fulfilling part of your life, but you may have trouble letting them go as they get older. This is your mothering instinct again dominating you.

You'd far rather give than receive and this is one area you need to overcome so others can enjoy the same pleasure of giving as you do. Learn to accept what is offered in the spirit of appreciation.

You'll always be on the go taking care of your family and friends, but don't forget to look after yourself and continue to improve on these areas that can undermine you emotionally. The most important person you need to demonstrate your love to at times is yourself.

Cancer man

Being born under Cancer doesn't diminish your masculinity in any way, even though it may make you more sensitive than the average bloke. Your protective exterior, however, will only scare people off for a short while because, once they get to know you a little more, they'll quickly see this softer side to your nature.

Powerful men like Harrison Ford, Nelson Mandela and, would you believe, George W. Bush, are all Cancers who exhibit this powerful masculine aspect to their characters but who are also deeply sensitive.

You always have something to say on any topic and, even if you're not particularly well versed in the subject of discussion, you tend to have a knack of making some vital contributions. You don't necessarily have to have a formal education, either, to show just what a wide range of knowledge you have. Cancer men seem to be eternal students who are constantly absorbing facts and different titbits of information.

Most women would be extremely happy to have someone like a Cancer man as part of their life, particularly if they're interested in a man who will enjoy family life with them. You'll make a great husband, father, get top marks as a homemaker and you're even a pretty good hand in the kitchen.

At times you're a little old-fashioned in the way you live your life but no one could accuse you of lacking in integrity. Your temperamental nature can be a problem but people should just leave you alone when you're feeling these mood swings.

You're a very determined person but your professional life may not go all that smoothly, especially in the earlier part of your life. Try to enjoy the process rather than focusing too much on the end goal. Patience, being one of your better traits, will help see you through these initial obstacles so success will eventually be yours.

If you're too soft and easygoing with people, they may take advantage of you from time to time. You'll need to learn to be just that little bit harder in your dealings with others and let them know where you stand.

The Cancer male is able to handle much more than the average person and can usually take on fairly large projects—some that others would cringe at. You're methodical and painstaking in your attention to detail. There are some Cancer men who will climb the ladder of success, but for the most part this will only be important if your personal and family life are not jeopardised in the process. You have one of the highest standards when it comes to your personal affairs.

For women who are involved with men born under Cancer you'll be surprised when you find out just how sensitive they are. They can be emotionally very intense and in the extreme a little too moody, especially if you're a woman that likes her own space. Closeness and security are important components of his life so don't take this as anything other than another expression of Cancer's love.

Cancer child

The Cancer child is a unique creature and, although sensitive, shy and sometimes a little emotionally inaccessible, you mustn't let that fool you as to their depth and level of understanding. At times they are misunderstood but on the whole they usually are well-behaved children and enjoy being part of the family dynamic.

Tread gently when rearing your Cancer child. Move softly and slowly in your approach, especially when correcting them on their errors because they are hypersensitive to criticism and may withdraw if you are a little too heavy handed. If you must take them to task, back it up with loads of kisses and cuddles and you'll achieve a much more productive response from them.

Some Cancer children are deprived of love at an early stage and it's not that all children don't need love, it's just that the Cancer child seems to need more of it and more consistently.

If your Cancer baby is not happy they will brood and bottle up their feelings and you may be none the wiser, so it's best to remain alert to the changing patterns of their moods. You'll soon get a handle on just how deep and complex they really are.

Cancer children are imaginative and inquisitive. Being ruled by the watery Moon, they like to be around ponds, lakes, rivers and the ocean, generally making excellent swimmers. They love exploring the vegetation and animal life that surrounds these places so try to cultivate their imagination by playing with them and allowing their aspirations to soar.

Cancer boys and girls love to be in the kitchen cooking, so you should expect somewhat of a mess to develop as they crawl in and out of every nook and cranny pulling the place to pieces but feeling they are part of the cooking process. I only hope you're not a Virgo parent who loves a meticulously tidy environment, even while cooking!

Art and music are excellent ways in which to bring peace and tranquillity to your child's moods and are areas in which their imagination can be developed. If you have a Cancer daughter she'll like playing with dolls and dolls' houses, while the boys will also join in and play the role of father with their mates.

Set clear boundaries for your teenage Cancer, especially in friendship. Because they have a strong need to be loved and be the centre of attention they'll go to great lengths to be accepted. Teach them moderation in their food as well, as Cancer is one of the star signs prone to putting on those kilos rather easily.

Romance, love and marriage

The quickest way to a Cancer heart is lots of cuddles and TLC; they'll keep coming back for more. Warmth and affection are their currency and, as long as they are reciprocated in this way, they'll feel reasonably comfortable in the relationship.

Because Cancer dominates the area of family and domestic issues, home life and associated activities will be of paramount importance. As long as your partner is committed to creating and fostering a loyal and devoted family, you'll be happy to consider that person your life and soulmate.

There are no half measures in your relationship once someone wins your heart. You're in it for the long haul and marriage to you is an honourable tradition. It's not unusual to find young Cancer girls idealising marriage and family life and you may have had these dreams, too. It doesn't mean you can't have a professional path as well, but you'll always try to find balance between your personal ambitions and love.

You're an excellent life partner because your sincerity and affection are genuine and your partner will never be in doubt as to how you feel about them. Some Cancers also have the touch of Scorpio in them and this therefore makes you a little possessive and jealous at times. Your reasoning, however, is that because you give your 'all', you expect the same in return.

Because of your powerful intuitive nature, you sense the moods and states of mind of your lovers. You also know when they are not being particularly honest with you. This can be a little unsettling for them and therefore they'll soon learn that honesty will have to be part and parcel of the relationship, otherwise you'll quickly show them the door.

Because you're so sensitive you often feel hurt and this in turn can lead you to bottle up your emotions when it's probably better to talk about how you feel.

Don't be scared to talk about how you feel and share your feelings because this can be a source of health issues for you, not to mention the fact that your relationships may suffer, too. Don't let your emotions reach boiling point before spilling the beans.

You need someone who can love you equally and with mutual respect. If you feel as though you're giving more than you receive, this will prove to be a problem. Sure, you are selfless, but there are limits as well. Hooking up with the earth signs or water signs is a good idea if you want a mate that will understand you on this level. Look at the compatibility section to get more details on that.

Being ruled by the Moon also means you can study your feelings by being aware of the lunar cycle. If you recognise these emotional signals early you can get on top of them and help avert some of the problems that are likely to arise between you and your loved ones.

Sometimes your partner will feel as if you're changeable and just too moody for their liking. Perhaps part of the problem is that, if you're bottling up your feelings, your lover or spouse may see this as pulling back, which in turn will cause them to pull back as well and thus the vicious cycle begins. The importance of not transmitting the wrong signals can't be overestimated here. Remember that not everyone is as complex as you and also not able to deal with your moodiness.

Being a little shy and withdrawn, you need to explain to others that this is not really who you are. For some Cancers who have been emotionally hurt in a previous relationship, your tough exterior may get tougher and tougher, making it hard for new people to break through to your inner self. This is a little counterproductive because closeness is really what you do desire in life.

You are the most loyal and faithful of people and, if you accept someone as a friend, you make them part of your inner circle, preferring a few close friends rather than many half-hearted acquaintances. To you, friendships are for life and you'll go the extra mile to prove your loyalty to them as well.

Health, wellbeing and diet

Your emotional sensitivity, health and physical vitality are very much linked. Your wellbeing will be dependent upon how well you manage your reactions to your environment and social and personal relationships.

Cancer is at times fragile health-wise, particularly in the earlier years, but your vitality usually strengthens with age.

In your desire to help people with emotional problems, you could easily get sucked down into the whirlpool of their emotional abyss, which in turn can affect you physically. Set some emotional boundaries when it comes to helping those in need so you don't end up becoming the victim in the process.

Cancer rules the chest, stomach and breasts. These parts of your body can be constitutionally a little weak from diseases or ailments such as coughs and colds. If you suffer from asthma and other bronchial disorders, it could be that some of the emotional issues we've discussed above are expressing themselves physically in you. Keep yourself warm in the cooler months and deal with some of these past issues. You'll overcome these problems and live a much more satisfactory life.

You love eating—and also growing, gathering and preparing it; actually, anything to do with the palate, especially with some socialising and preparation involved—but I would suggest a little moderation, Cancer.

Rich, sumptuous food is definitely on the top of your menu. 'The richer, the better' seems to be your motto, but it is not necessarily going to work for you in the long term. I suggest you try something a little less laden with kilojoules and you can do this with some imagination and investigation.

You could try white and pink fruits such as honeydew melons, banana and some of the lighter coloured fruits such as lemons. These are excellent tonics as well as cleansing your system.

White vegetables such as squash and potatoes are also good, but try not to eat your carbs too late in the day. Bake your vegetables and reduce your butter and fat intake. These accessory kilojoules are where you can make a special effort and, while still enjoying your food, you will be pleased to see you don't put on extra kilos.

Low-fat cottage cheese, cucumbers, lettuce and other salads are also great for your metabolism. Try including some calming herb teas such as chamomile to help with mood swings and getting more restful sleep.

Work

Above all, your work must be a means of expressing your love and your care for others and also a way of keeping your family safe and secure.

You're responsible and dependable in your approach to most matters and your employment will be no exception. With a comfortable workplace, you can be reasonably creative doing great work and earning a good living from it. You might even like to work from home as many Cancers start out doing a hobby and develop it into a profitable business.

Care and attention to detail is important to you and if you're a team player you like to be part of the process from inception to completion. You love sharing the results with others but you must guard against being too patronising as you often feel that you are the one who knows best.

Money will always be important to you as it offers the stability and security that is necessary for a comfortable life in which you can nurture the ones you love. Banking and real estate are also areas that fit this side of your nature.

The best careers for Cancers include professions such as nursing, counselling and other medical fields. Cooking, catering and hospitality would give you a great sense of satisfaction as well.

Because Cancer rules the sea, many Cancers also do well working in professions connected with the ocean, sailing, cruise ships and resorts.

Your lucky days

Your luckiest days are Mondays, Tuesdays, Thursdays and Sundays.

Your lucky numbers

Remember that the forecasts given later in the book will help you optimise your chances of winning. Your lucky numbers are:

2, 11, 20, 29, 38, 47

9, 18, 27, 36, 45, 54

3, 12, 21, 30, 48, 57

Your destiny years

Your most important years are 2, 11, 20, 29, 38, 47, 56, 74 and 83.

Star Sign
Compatibility

What man really seeks is not perfection, which is in the future,
but fulfilment, which is ever in the present.

—N. Sri Ram

Romantic compatibility

How compatible are you with your current partner, lover or friend? Did you know that astrology can reveal a whole new level of understanding between people simply by looking at their star sign and that of their partner? In this chapter I'd like to share some special insights that will help you better appreciate your strengths and challenges using Sun sign compatibility.

The Sun reflects your drive, willpower and personality. The essential qualities of two star signs blend like two pure colours producing an entirely new colour. Relationships, similarly, produce their own emotional colours when two people interact. The following is a general guide to your romantic prospects with others and how, by knowing the astrological 'colour' of each other, the art of love can help you create a masterpiece.

When reading the following I ask you to remember that no two star signs are ever *totally* incompatible. With effort and compromise, even the most 'difficult' astrological matches can work. Don't close your mind to the full range of life's possibilities! Learning about each other and ourselves is the most important facet of astrology.

Each star sign combination is followed by the elements of those star signs and the result of their combining. For instance, Aries is a fire sign and Aquarius is an air sign, and this combination produces a lot of 'hot air'. Air feeds fire, and fire warms air. In fact, fire requires air. However, not all air and fire combinations work. I have included information about the different birth periods within each star sign and this will throw even more light on your prospects for a fulfilling love life with any star sign you choose.

Good luck in your search for love, and may the stars shine upon you in 2009!

Compatibility quick reference guide

Each of the twelve star signs has a greater or lesser affinity with one another. The quick reference guide on page 30 will show you who's hot and who's not so hot as far as your relationships are concerned.

CANCER + ARIES
Water + Fire = Steam

It might not seem like a great match at first but Cancer and Aries have some mutually useful energies that can enhance both their lives. Some Cancerians are immediately attracted to Aries because they see in them all the warmth and vitality they would like to have.

Aries happens to fall at the zenith of the horoscope for you, Cancer, and this means there is something in them that you aspire to and respect. Even if the elements of water and fire, which rule both your signs respectively, seem to be diametrically opposed, the fire of Aries will warm your heart, your deeper emotions, and you can possibly tone down the bright fires of Aries with your soothing and cooling waters.

You may choose to enter into a deep and meaningful relationship with Aries and, if you do, you'll need to be prepared to lift your energy levels to incredibly new heights to keep up with them. Arians are fast, intense and always on the go, but you'll want to do this too because both signs are changeable, cardinal, and this indicates a lot of movement and progress for both of you. You're certainly a little less intense than your

Quick reference guide: Horoscope compatibility between signs (percentage)

	Pisces	Aquarius	Capricorn	Sagittarius	Scorpio	Libra	Virgo	Leo	Cancer	Gemini	Taurus	Aries
Aries	65	55	50	90	80	70	45	90	65	65	65	60
Taurus	85	80	95	50	85	75	90	70	80	70	70	70
Gemini	50	90	50	75	60	90	75	80	60	75	70	70
Cancer	90	70	45	55	95	60	75	70	75	60	80	65
Leo	75	70	45	95	75	65	75	85	70	80	70	90
Virgo	70	50	95	70	85	80	70	75	75	75	90	45
Libra	50	95	85	80	85	80	80	65	60	90	75	70
Scorpio	95	60	65	80	90	85	85	75	95	60	85	80
Sagittarius	75	60	55	85	85	80	70	95	55	75	50	90
Capricorn	85	70	85	55	65	85	95	45	45	50	95	50
Aquarius	55	80	70	60	60	95	50	70	70	90	80	55
Pisces	80	55	85	75	95	50	55	75	90	50	85	65

Aries partner but this doesn't necessarily mean the match can't work.

Financially you could work well together with the industriousness of Aries combining well with your intuitive feelings. It also shows a great match in terms of family life. Your nurturing attitude is perfect for Aries, while the Aries' protective aspect makes you feel safe and secure.

Your sexual attitudes are a little different. You would like to see more sensitivity and less bravado on the part of Aries. They are impulsive and want quick and spontaneous results in the bedroom. Yet, if the Arian partner we are talking about is the 'Wham, bam, thank you ma'am' type, it's hardly likely to be a long-term and fulfilling relationship, is it?

Although not an ideal match, you do have some strong links with those Aries born between 21 and 30 March. You could become good friends and spiritually advise each other.

If you team up with someone born between 31 March and 10 April, they are co-ruled by the Sun, which dominates your finances. You can work well together and earn considerable money in your association with them, but it's not likely to be the best romantic match. If it's status and financial security you're after, then maybe this is your soulmate.

Other Arians born between 11 and 20 April can be challenging to you, even though Jupiter is considered friendly to both of your star signs. Unless Aries is grounded and practical, you might not feel all that comfortable spending time in a long-term relationship with them. They will need to satisfy your domestic needs for a nurturing and loving environment. This last group of Aries can also be a little egotistical and preoccupied with themselves. They are very independent and may not easily settle down.

CANCER + TAURUS

Water + Earth = Mud

Both Cancer and Taurus are primarily interested in security and, being female signs of the zodiac, are very receptive to each other and generally this is a promising association.

Certainly, Cancer, you'll enjoy a quality lifestyle, but for Taurus to think money is on the top of your security agenda, would be a serious mistake. To you money is only part of the mix and not as important as the emotional connection, and you must be careful not to confuse the emotional security that you require with the financial and material security of Taurus.

Taurus can anchor you in life and, because at times you are changeable and moody, they have a certain sobering effect on you by soothing your tensions. However, Taurus women can also at times be moody (not so much with the men). If this is the case, this could be a challenge for both of you and can bring about reactive squabbles from time to time. Fortunately you are able to overcome this rather quickly and get the relationship back on the straight and narrow.

In the esoteric scheme of astrology, the water signs are considered as more spiritually evolved. This means that your insights can actually work without too much of a hitch on the Taurus temperament to effect important changes in their lives.

You're a practical person, especially where it comes to your family and close friends. This is one aspect of your character that Taurus respects because they too don't mind getting their hands dirty and actually doing things. Sexually you have friendly planets ruling this part of your life so I foresee your moments of intimacy bringing you both a great deal of satisfaction.

Taurus falls in the realm of friendship astrologically and therefore you can both get on very well as friends, especially with those born between 11 and 21 May. I see a relationship with these Taureans as allowing you both to build a secure and very bonding relationship. They in particular will understand your mind and be able to calm you emotionally.

Domestic and financial security will be offered by them and this will provide you with all-round satisfaction. Mind you, they're not exactly the most spontaneous of people but I think these other good qualities far outweigh this one shortcoming.

Taureans born between 21 and 29 April can start out well but may lose momentum as time goes on. This is not the best of combinations and you may need to be careful that they also don't work against your better interests. You'll need to develop your lines of communication together and share your ideas as this will be a key factor in bridging any gap you may have.

If you happen to be a male Cancer, Taurean women may draw you into lavishing gifts and spending inordinate amounts of money on them. Even though Taureans are usually financially independent enough to make their own way, make sure you both have a clear understanding of your financial commitment to each other.

Taureans born between 30 April and 10 May appeal to you because they have a great sense of humour. The two of you will enjoy each other's company and can look forward to a great social life together.

CANCER + GEMINI
Water + Air = Rain

You're ruled by the Moon, which reflects your changing, sensitive and emotional nature. You're a feeler rather than a thinker, absorbing the vibrations of your environment and the people in it. Gemini on the other hand is ruled by Mercury. This shows that their thinking and reasoning is highly developed and so they have a tendency to deal with their world using their brains.

The result is that there is quite a difference in the way you approach life, and each other. You need to work hard at bridging this gap if you want to enter a serious relationship and accept each other for who you are.

Gemini is so preoccupied intellectually that it's hard to get them to be in touch with their feelings. You will need to exhibit a high level of intellectual curiosity, even though you are an emotional being. Gemini takes pride intellectually and needs this to sustain them in their personal relationships.

If the Gemini you have in mind is a little more patient than your typical astrological 'twin', you might be able to lure them slowly into the world of feelings and intuition to which they are usually unaccustomed. They too can maybe show you the way out of your occasional moodiness and temperamental ways. This therefore could be a win/win situation if you're both prepared to learn and grow together.

You have extraordinary psychic abilities and this could be one way in which you could make a real connection with them. Gemini may be a little sceptical but will not be able to dismiss your uncanny ability to tune into what they're thinking and doing. They may be so impressed they might try to follow suit and get in touch with their own inner being.

There's certainly a sexual lure towards Gemini and the two of you can have some humorous times together during your most intimate moments. Laughter would have to be your best common denominator. Using this as a foundation, your sexual lives will be all the richer for it.

Be careful financially with Geminis born between 22 May and 1 June. You have differences in your attitudes to money, which need to be sorted out early in the relationship. Share your ideas about what it really means to you and this should bypass some of the problems between Cancer and Gemini.

Those Gemini born between 2 and 12 June tend to offer you loads of fun socially and this is because Venus influences the relationship. You're attracted to these individuals because they have strong ambitions and sensual magnetism.

There's also a very strong sexual attraction to Geminis born between 13 and 21 June. Don't let your physical attraction override your need for emotional and material commitment from them. Gemini is a very flighty sign of the zodiac and sometimes doesn't offer you the security and stability you're after.

Being with a Gemini will no doubt be exciting but a compromise will be the keyword for both of you to make this match mutually satisfying.

CANCER + CANCER
Water + Water = Deluge

Relationships should always be based on mutual understanding and emotional nourishment. Fortunately, your star sign coupled with a person born under the same one means you instinctively understand where you're both coming from.

Your ideals in life with another Cancer are also on par as you both believe that family life, children and working for the good of domestic happiness is well worth it. You're receptive to the other and, because Cancer is often a selfless sign, you're interested in relieving each other's problems.

You're both receptive to the feelings of others; however, this might not always be advantageous because you may draw the negative vibrations of each other just at a time you're feeling quite good and lowering your energy to the level of the other. Beware of this trap.

Two water signs can sometimes be emotionally overpowering. You'll need to step back and be unbiased in what you feel are decisions that need to be made for the good of the relationship. If you're too emotionally involved in each other's problems, this could be hard.

Growing a family will be one of the primary motivations for you as a couple, and if you've been involved for some time, this is one feature of each other's character that will make you very happy.

The sexual relationship is based upon what it should be; that is, being caring, sensitive and demonstrative towards each other. Because of this you feel a strong sense of security and love and this resonates well between you. Whether you are male or female doesn't really matter much because the Moon, which is your ruler, is feminine and thereby prompts even the men born under this sign to be very much in tune with their feminine side.

Because the sign of Aquarius dominates your sexual attitudes, it might be surprising to learn that most Cancerians are quite prepared to explore their sexuality in ways that aren't so traditional and this could make your love life very exciting.

Cancer rules home life, the home and the domestic sphere and you'll both enjoy cooking, gardening and hanging around the house together. You'll find comfort and consolation while doing things at home and are not bothered that the other doesn't want much of a social life.

One of the strongest connections you could have is with a Cancer born between 14 and 23 July. This combination of Cancer promises a fortunate destiny. The double-rulership of the Moon can challenge your basic compatibility, though, as you'll react a little too strongly to each other. Just try to tune in to what you have in common rather than point out each other's flaws.

You'll do well in family life together and children will be an important component of this.

Cancers born between 22 June and 3 July can be exceedingly emotional and over-reactive. Sex will be an important part of the relationship because of the powerful Scorpio influence. Deep, intense and sensual affections are connected to them. They may be a little dominating and, if you're prepared to take the back seat, this match can also work.

Cancer born between 4 and 13 July are also a good match and they too offer you plenty of sexual satisfaction.

CANCER + LEO
Water + Fire = Steam

Cancer, ruled by the Moon, and Leo, ruled by the Sun, will act in much the same way when in a partnership. The Sun and Leo, with their dramatic displays of showiness, will project their energy onto and through you, Cancer.

The Leo-born person will augment your life, making you feel happy and more enriched. Certainly, you'll probably be overwhelmed by the enthusiastic and competent character; but this is ideal, especially if you lack confidence and need to lift your spirits. Leo will do that for you.

Leo is extremely demonstrative and loyal in relationships and they will appreciate you for who you are. Sometimes, too, the Moon and the Sun come together and the light is completely obscured in an eclipse. Therefore, there are two extremes in this relationship; but overall I see this working in the way the traditional and classic astrologers have expressed. The Moon and the Sun are male and female archetypes, and therefore this can be a 'match made in heaven'.

Leo is also a fire sign and can warm the cockles of your heart. But, they are also extremely independent people. Although family oriented, they need to be assured by you that they can have the best of both worlds; that is, a nurturing and comfortable family life and also an independent lifestyle where they can shine and bring out their best creative self.

Leo is the centre of attention, just like the Sun, it being the centre of the solar system. They need constant approval, constant pampering, love and nurturing, and who better than Cancer to give this to them? Be careful you don't spoil them!

The best combination of Cancer and Leo is between those born between 15 and 23 August. It's likely you'll meet them through a work-related activity, but this also has some elements of secrecy associated with it. Some Leos and Cancers work together and then become sexually infatuated, as in the case of a boss–employee scenario. That's to be expected because of the high level of attraction between you and the passionate and intense character of Leo.

Leos born between 24 July and 4 August are strongly connected to your material sense of values. They bring you good financial and commercial luck, and this might be a little too hard to resist because you must agree that having love and wealth is not a bad combination.

Your energies blend very well and you stimulate their ambitions. They like to demonstrate their love by presenting you with gifts and other material favours. If money, status and power are the things you crave, then these Leo born individuals will definitely fulfil your dreams.

Those born between 5 and 14 August have Jupiter as their co-ruler, which means they're not altogether that compatible. They are big thinkers; dreamers who sometimes appear to be out of touch with practical reality. You mightn't feel as secure as you'd like to be with them but they'll give you a good time with their spontaneity and easy attitude.

CANCER + VIRGO

Water + Earth = Mud

This combination of star signs is one of the better ones in the zodiac, with the two of your signs being feminine and in good positions to each other.

Your sensitive ruler, the Moon, and the bright spark of the zodiac, Mercury, which rules Virgo, combine to bring you many interesting times ahead. Cancer falls in the zone of friendship for Virgo and will always feel your loyalty and support, which draws them to you very closely. Virgo has some difficulty understanding the intense Cancerian mood swings because they are primarily rational individuals. They tend to think about their feelings whereas you tend to feel your thoughts.

Although these seem like diametrically opposed perspectives, you can still be compatible with Virgo. Virgo is responsive and exceedingly communicative. They like to reason things through, even if it is something unpalatable, and will not walk away when you're talking to them. Virgos like balance and within themselves need resolution. This will endear them to you as you have a similar way of seeing things.

The combination of your star signs brings about considerable imagination and this can be pleasurable for you as you're likely to come up with the most left-of-field solutions. You're both talented in your own different way and the combination of these strengths is a plus for the relationship.

Few can withstand the critical nature of Virgo, but you're one star sign that may indeed weather the storms of nitpicking. Even though you are a little vulnerable and sensitive, let's not forget that the crab does have a hard exterior (even though soft on the inside) and must protect itself when considering the valuable insights Virgo has to offer.

Sexually your attitudes are a little different and again the precision of Virgo may seem too contrived for your natural, emotional and tactile approach. You must break down the earthy habits of Virgo with your sensual waters of love. You can do it and achieve a much greater level of sexual satisfaction together.

There are difficulties in communication with Virgos born between 24 August and 2 September. Although strongly influenced by Mercury they are not the chatterboxes that you might prefer. They have a tendency to be ruthlessly critical of you and themselves, but in your company they'll slowly learn to be a little gentler and appreciate the positive side of their own personalities. You'll be doing them a great service if you do so.

Virgos born between 3 and 12 September are quite suitable as marriage partners with a strong bond between you both emotionally and sexually. Take your time, however, as they don't open their hearts as quickly as most. You wouldn't want to overlook this more sensitive side to their character. They'll also be capable of giving you the financial security you so desire.

Good friendship can be expected with Virgos born between 13 and 23 September. They can make you laugh, but at the same time have an extraordinary knowledge of general facts and figures. You'll be constantly stimulated by them.

CANCER + LIBRA
Water + Air = Rain

Cancer and Libra are cardinal signs and astrologically form a right-angle in the heavens. This right-angle or square aspect is a challenge and shows that if the two of you enter into a relationship you can expect some important life-altering changes to occur with each other.

In a Cancer–Libra combination we see that if you're prepared to withstand the discomfort of these challenges, you can break through and achieve peace, harmony and some valuable spiritual growth from the contact.

You like a retiring, peaceful and domestic situation in which to thrive. Against the backdrop of Libra's social nature, you might feel somewhat mismatched with their continual pleasure seeking and need for variety. If you're in a relationship with a Libran, you have to motivate yourself to look beyond the comfort of the moment and explore the social horizons Libra can introduce you to.

The planets ruling your marital lives are also very different. You have a more traditional and conservative approach to marriage whereas Libra may need to play the field a little more and is obviously progressive compared with you. The intimacy factor between Cancer and Libra is good on one level, though, because the female planets of the Moon and Venus rule your signs, respectively. Libra is a masculine sign and therefore you might not always see the underlying sensitivity that is always there in a Libra. You need to get on the same wavelength as your Libran partner and show them that you're prepared to explore life with them. This can encourage them in moving forward with you in love.

The additional benefit of these two female planets ruling you is that there should be sexual compatibility between you. This could be the one saving grace and, even though your marital planets are not so harmonious, you can have considerable fun between the sheets.

Librans born between 24 September and 3 October are great companions and offer you the best of advice. Librans are master communicators and also have a way of balancing the problems of others. You'll feel they are supportive of you in your time of need and you appreciate this.

You could feel uptight with Librans born between 4 and 13 October, but sexually you're still attracted to them. This is a typical love/hate relationship you've probably heard about where you find yourself swinging between the extremes of great love and utter frustration. They're quite demanding and can eventually use up many of your resources—particularly emotional ones.

You have to state the boundaries with these Librans. Your tendency to want to help everyone only means you'll become a victim in the end and then this will reveal the worst side of their character. They'll respect you more if you state your case up-front.

Tread carefully with Librans born between 14 and 23 October as well. You mustn't let money rule the relationship and also make sure you keep tabs on who is spending what. This could turn into a battle of wills over who controls the purse strings.

You're quite prudent and economical compared to this lot, who like luxury and have no trouble spending money—theirs or your own. Take control of your financial future and this will ensure long-term stability for the relationship as well.

CANCER + SCORPIO
Water + Water = Deluge

It's important for zodiac elements to agree if you would like to get on with a partner and have a good chance of the relationship working. Both Cancer and Scorpio, being water elements, fall under this category. This endows you both with sensitivity, emotionalism and intuitive capacity. You are tuned in to each other and can express your love in the way each of you wishes.

You must be prepared for the demanding and sometimes difficult relationship when becoming involved with a Scorpio. But that will be of little concern when you fall head over heels in love with them. Scorpio is notorious for hypnotic eyes that can mesmerise and draw the Cancerian into their powerful orb. You have the ability to lessen the intensity of Scorpio so that they're able to open their hearts and allow you a glimpse of their true self.

Scorpio will appreciate your nurturing and attentive quality in the relationship but they do tend to be a bottomless pit as far as love and sex are concerned. Cancer, to them, is certainly one of the few signs to whom they can feel comfortable in giving their 'all'.

This is the proverbial 'love at first sight' combination and a love affair with Scorpio has all the hallmarks of excitement, passion and also long-term durability. Sexually you are quite different but the planets ruling this area of activity are quite well suited and indicate that you're both playful and also open to variety and exploration.

It is indeed love at first sight with Scorpios born between 24 October and 2 November. Both of you feel sensually enhanced in each other's company and astrologically this is probably the best match with a Scorpio. Something in this type of Scorpio brings out the best flavour of your Cancerian nurturing quality. You're able to recreate Scorpio and make them better people.

Scorpios born between 3 and 12 November have strong philosophical interests but will also want to share and protect their higher knowledge with you. You have deeper connections with them and you'll both learn a great deal from each other. They are like gurus to you and you're attracted to them because you feel your mutual giving will ennoble the human spirit as well.

You have a good feeling when in contact with Scorpios born between 13 and 22 November. You're able to draw out their softer emotional side and you feel somehow that your destiny and theirs are meant to coincide. Working together with them to help and generally uplift other people is a great cause, but you shouldn't allow it to dominate your relationship.

CANCER + SAGITTARIUS

Water + Fire = Steam

You mustn't under any circumstance cringe under the larger-than-life Sagittarian character. They would expect you to hold your own with them and this is really a matter of belief.

You're somewhat in awe of the popular, easygoing and optimistic Sagittarian, whose adventurous lifestyle is probably quite different to what you had imagined you'd like for your own future, right? But if you enjoy travel and mixing with and meeting people with diverse interests, this proposition will start to seem more and more attractive as time goes on.

Sagittarius is the sixth sign to Cancer, which is not considered all that compatible, even though your ruling planets do have good rapport with each other. Their high level of energy could drain you of your own essential life force and might leave you feeling energetically depleted.

You like Sagittarius's honest—blunt and yes insensitive at times—but nevertheless straight-down-the-line attitude, which is how you'd prefer it. You'll always know where you stand with them.

They love to be out and about, free like the wind; whereas you'd like something far more anchored, especially in the family scene.

Sagittarius is attracted to your sensitivity and sensual receptivity and this is one of the partnership's strengths. Sagittarius will need to exhibit a little more patience with you to make you feel completely comfortable. Feel your way through this for a while before giving your body, mind and soul to them. Your temperaments are really quite different and you'll need time to develop an intimate relationship with them.

Sagittarians born between 23 November and 1 December are sometimes friendly and at other times quite the opposite.

They are enigmas in your book as you won't know how to figure them out. Before you get too involved with them try to establish what their motives and life goals are. Trust will be a slow process with them, so take your time.

You could be seduced by the excitement of the moment only to find that these individuals are just a little too hot to handle. As long as you're asking questions, you won't put a foot wrong; but if you dive in boots and all you may find you're out of your depth.

Sagittarians born between 2 and 11 December are a very good match for you. There's a high degree of compatibility with them and marriage and long-term love are quite likely.

This is one group of Sagittarians that stand out from the rest as being particularly well suited to your temperament. They are able to do things differently and have an original spin on things. You need to have your bags packed for spur of the moment travels with them, but it will always be an exciting relationship, nonetheless.

There's a financial level of compatibility with Sagittarians born between 12 and 22 December. Although you are attracted to their personality, they are probably wedded to their work and financial commitments.

CANCER + CAPRICORN
Water + Earth = Mud

Cancer and Capricorn are opposite zones of the zodiac so naturally there is an attraction between you right from the outset, but be prepared for some differences that you should iron out before getting too involved with them.

Capricorn's cool and undemonstrative attitude might lead you to believe that they are in no way attracted to or even in the least bit interested in you, but they are not exactly the best at expressing those feelings of love and warmth. Don't assume that they feel no attraction for you because it's quite likely they are seething inside with passion but unable to articulate it.

Tokens of their affection are shown in the way they give gifts, provide security with money, and the way they like to plan for the future and include you in these plans. If they mention this to you, take it as a given that you are very much close to their heart and that they wish you to be part of their lives.

Capricorn measures their emotional wellbeing by what they have. This can also be applied to their family values too but you might find they put their financial and material interests ahead of their emotional commitment. This is just a different perspective on your part and not necessarily completely true.

Don't let this relationship become one of convenience, of bartering or exchanging goods for emotional favours. Make sure you're both clear on what you want from the other and, if necessary, push Capricorn beyond their limits because usually they don't want to discuss some of these confrontational issues. But, they must.

Sexually and emotionally your signs are very different, with your personality demanding more from the restrained Capricorn than they can provide. You have to be very clever in working your way into their hearts, to nudge them into satisfying your needs, but a warm and responsive being awaits you. It can be done, but it could be an arduous task.

Marriage or a permanent bond of friendship is quite likely with Capricorns born between 23 December and 1 January. This is a powerful relationship in which you're both strongly attracted to each other. A serious and stable Capricorn makes you feel grounded and secure. Capricorns sometimes appear older than their years and in fact you may even attract someone a little older in this group. If you've had difficult issues with your parents as a child you might be attracted to an older Capricorn as a substitute parent in some way.

Capricorns born between 2 and 10 January are a really good match for you. They can fulfil you physically and you'll feel inspired mentally. There is also a creative connection between you and these Capricorns and therefore art, music and drama may feature strongly in your relationship.

The sexual chemistry between you and Capricorns born between 11 and 20 January is very powerful, but make sure that this is not simply fun and superficial because at times your emotional approach to these Capricorns will help them gain a greater insight into their own emotional being.

CANCER + AQUARIUS
Water + Air = Rain

Some Aquarians are quite wild, loving their freedom and independence and are therefore quite different to the typical Cancer. Aquarians love to do things on the spur of the moment, impromptu, always with a little shock value thrown in.

It's often hard for Aquarius to settle down, especially in the first part of their lives, but you may be able to seduce them into your cosy, loving home space. You'll soothe their soul and this will pull you closer together.

You'd have to be a very special Cancer to put an end to the independent Aquarian's need for freedom. They need to explore the highways and byways of life before firmly committing to someone, but if you're prepared to put aside your conservative approach to the relationship, you might get some mileage out of a love affair.

This unusual astrological combination brings together the lunar vibrations of Cancer and the eclectic Uranian element of

Aquarius. This can produce rather unexpected and often high-tension effects.

You like to know what's happening day by day, and be fore-warned of a change in plans, but Aquarius may leave you exasperated with their abrupt and often unexpected changes in their schedules. However, this could be the perfect opportunity for you to explore life and take in some extraordinary experiences with them.

Sexually your relationship with Aquarius will be passionate and exciting because your star sign falls in their sexual zone; however, you have different styles. They are rather intellectual and often aloof in much of what they do and sex may also be included in that.

Aquarians born between 21 and 30 January can be trouble-some in your life. The initial excitement you feel could end up burning you out in the long run. They are unsettled and seek out extreme excitement and new and novel experiences, so their unpredictability could throw you off course. This is not really what you're after in a relationship, but if you want to break free from your typical day-to-day routine, they could be the answer.

Can you keep up with an Aquarian born between 31 January and 8 February? If you enjoy getting out and about, you'll be able to be part of their routine and this will help the relationship immensely by giving you something in common. In some cases, a Cancer–Aquarian relationship with people born during this period may see you relocating to a com-pletely different area. You might find yourself having to choose between staying where you are with the people you know or following your romantic dreams with them.

You'll completely identify with people born between 9 and 19 February. You'll feel tremendous love for these Aquar-ians and your friendship will be based upon their wacky but harmlessly mad behaviour. You love the fact that they're different. These Aquarians tend to have a slightly more settled lifestyle than others born at this time of the year, which gives you satisfaction in terms of excitement and likely domestic stability.

CANCER + PISCES
Water + Water = Deluge

Star signs of the same element are destined to get on well but in this case a little too much water may not always work that favourably.

Pisces is particularly prone to having its head in the clouds, to idealising life and seeing life through the rosiest-coloured pair of glasses, but they can lose sight of all practicality, according to you, Cancer.

You certainly feel emotionally close and bond well on that idealistic level, having an instinctive understanding of each other's needs. You're both caring and supportive, but Pisces is sometimes out of touch and in their own little world.

As well, the watery emotions of Cancer are best expressed through the domestic and immediate family needs that are so much reflected by the sign of Cancer. Alternatively, Pisces' emotional expression is directed more to a spiritual and universal means, which is often too abstract for you to grasp.

However, there is a karmic link between you and, on the deepest level, you and Pisces are destined to grow together and slowly but surely can pull together as a team to balance the Piscean 'otherworldly' spiritual ideals with your family values and practical thinking.

Intimacy between you will be wonderful because you both understand that true love and compassion should underpin any type of physical relationship. Pisces feels this with you and you also sense that they very genuinely care about you. As a result your moments of intimacy will allow you both to open your hearts fully and experience an extraordinary level of passion, warmth and personal fulfilment.

You're likely to have a very close spiritual involvement with Pisces born between 20 and 28 February. These Pisces are sometimes a little too impractical for your tastes. Because your water sign of Cancer is earthy as well as grounded, you might just be able to lure them back to Earth and give them balance in their lives.

The best combination with Pisces is with those born between 1 and 10 March. They're extremely sensitive beings and will attract you very powerfully. At the outset of your meeting with them you'll feel as if you've known each other in some other life. It's also an excellent romantic combination due to the influence of the Moon on their lives. You'll both naturally provide for each other's needs and this is one of the better matches of the zodiac.

There's a very strong sexual attraction with Pisces born between 11 and 20 March. Be prepared for their demands, however, as they expect 100 per cent in return for their love. This also has to be considered one of the best combinations of the zodiac and so I predict a fulfilling relationship with them.

2009:
The Year Ahead

Start by doing what's necessary; then do what's possible; and suddenly you are doing the impossible.

—Francis of Assisi

Romance and friendship

You will remember the year 2009 as an extremely important one as far as your relationships and personal affairs are concerned. I can't stress enough just how important they will be but the planets do give me some indication and I'd like to share those insights with you here.

At the commencement of the year, no less than five planets, including the Sun, Mars and Jupiter join their energies in your marital zone so it's hardly surprising you will feel dynamic and ready and raring to go, romantically. You're ready to take the lead and make your relationships work to your advantage, not just to others. The tide will turn and you'll no longer feel like the proverbial doormat.

You are more communicative and likely to speak your mind rather than bottling up those feelings and brooding for lengthy periods. This might come as a shock to people who usually see you as the peacemaker, not prepared to upset the applecart and challenge them head on. But, 2009 is a new year and you realise it is time for a new you!

The new Moon occurs in your arena of sexuality and this will also be highlighted importantly in January. With Venus and Neptune nearby, you'll be projecting your fantasies and will also want to make them a reality.

In February, you'll take a punt and step outside your normal way of doing things, prepared to take a step in a bold, new direction. Outdated friendships will be due for a shake-up and your personal ideals will change markedly.

You might have to do a lot of explaining by going back over the past and examining your history with others. This will be more pronounced if you're married. Your spouse or partner may find it hard to adjust to these changes and I see this month possibly leading to some conflict if you're not able to explain the change in your behaviour.

Venus gives you an amazing amount of popularity and success as it drives its way through the upper part of your horoscope. In the sign of Aries it will make you restless, changeable and hungry for new affairs. It's likely your work will provide you with an environment in which you can foster some of these fantasies and suppressed desires. You'll be creative and on the lookout for like-minded friends and associates who can share your vision of an exciting new phase in your life.

Your popularity continues very strongly throughout March and April, but Venus in its retrogression might cause you to rethink some of your strategies, especially if you're acting out from your ego rather than a sense of solid values. Show without substance is not the best foundation on which to base any new friendships. Sooner or later an astute person will see through these games and I warn you to keep it real.

In April the new Moon takes place in your zone of friendships, social alliances and community values. You can turn over a new leaf but also at this time meet many new faces that make you feel worthy and confident for simply being who you are. You may meet someone born under the sign of Taurus or Capricorn and their practical sense of values will inspire you in some way. Their approach to problem solving and dealing with their own issues will make sense to you and this could accelerate your personal growth at this time.

Your marriage planet Saturn undergoes some very tough challenges from the planet Mars throughout April and you'll be severely tested. They say that what doesn't kill you only makes you stronger and this could be one of those times when you will feel that this maxim very much applies to your circumstances. Fortunately, Venus, the Sun and Mercury are able to help you withstand some of the demands that your personal and domestic life will bring you at this time. Uranus and Pluto will also have a say in carving up your traditional values by unsettling circumstances on the home front.

Your domestic planet is primarily Venus, and its association with Uranus in the early part of the year can bring disruptions from other family members or relatives who want to stick their nose into business that isn't theirs. It will become tricky if you have children or are associating with children whose parents have different sets of values. Keep the lines of communication open with your own kids and the parents of their friends so that confusion doesn't reign.

Passion is high up on your agenda throughout May when Venus and Mars come into contact. This is a contrast to the earlier challenges of Mars and Saturn and the pendulum may well swing in the completely opposite direction. Sex, lust and excitement are quite likely to be on offer for the middle part of the year. Mars also then activates your social activities again in June and there'll be nothing stopping you. This could even be hectic with Mercury introducing many new friendships, which require an additional amount of communication on your part. Expect loads of telephone calls, letters and other forms of correspondence.

The new Moon in July is important as it refreshes your self-image and brings with it a desire to set some new resolutions for yourself. The Sun is also growing in its brightness and shows your popularity has increased and your self-confidence will certainly replace any previous feelings of self-doubt. I suggest you take the time to talk with children or friends who are younger in age as there is a chance you may miss some vital signals which reflect some emotional challenges for them.

In August particularly you'll need to make yourself available to help them through several crises. Because of your caring and sensitive nature I'm sure you will be quick to pick up on any hints that are dropped.

September sees Mars dominating the celestial landscape with its presence in your Sun sign. You'll be physical, vital and particularly reactive, especially with the Moon in the opposite sign of Capricorn. You'll be shooting from the hip, much to your later regret. Listen a little more than you talk before casting judgement and your relationships will fare much better.

Venus, Mercury and Saturn join forces in your third zone of travels in October. This is the time of the year when you can shut the door behind you and head for the hills if time out is what you need. It's not a bad idea, because the conjunction of Venus and Saturn can often cool your passions and make this cycle a reflective one. The Sun is also challenging your relationships and this could mean you'll be at odds with your partner or significant other on domestic issues. A little time apart is not a bad idea at all.

An important transition takes place in November with the entry of Saturn into your zone of family life, domestics and personal happiness. This is not an easy transition and heralds the commencement of a two-and-a-half-year cycle in which many changes will take place in this arena of your life. Slow, steady and level-headed thinking is necessary and I advise against any dramatic displays or reactions that would be simply jumping the gun. If you've felt a deep-seated dissatisfaction in any personal matter, you need to continue to work through it and earn your way out of the relationship if you feel the story is over.

This transit also has reference to your early historical life and your parents; in particular, your mother. Your relationship with her may come to the fore at this time and, if you happen to be a middle-aged Cancerian, some extra responsibility is possible in the last part of the year. Meet these responsibilities head on and don't begrudge the fact that you may have to surrender some of your personal social activities to do so. You'll find great satisfaction in doing this, believe it or not, even if it's hard at first.

Venus moving through your fifth zone of love affairs, pleasures and sports means you'll be out and about in December. For unattached Cancerians this is a great time to 'put it out there' and use your emotional attractiveness to draw the right sort of person to you. There'll be nothing stopping you throughout Christmas as Venus is in an excellent position with a challenging but not so damaging Mars lending weight to this fact.

If you accept your personal responsibilities this year, it will bring you to a new level of understanding that will hold you in good stead as 2009 comes to completion. With added wisdom, insight and self-satisfaction, you'll be well equipped to move forward with a renewed sense of faith and optimism.

Work and money

Although Cancer is considered a domestic and oftentimes an introverted sign of the zodiac, dealing with people will be an inescapable fact of life during 2009; but this is great! The power of your zone of public relations is so strong that, even if you've been averse to dealing with others in the past, you'll get a taste for it this year and do very well in propelling your personal, professional and business interests as a result.

You'll have numerous good instincts this year, so trust them because they could be turned into solid gold through a little bit of know-how, discipline and careful execution of your plans.

Make sure you sort out your shared finances early in the year, clearly defining what's yours and what's theirs. This will save you problems later in the year.

The new Moon of March can signify a turning point for many Cancerians in their working lives. New job opportunities are what I see for you at this time and you'd be crazy not to investigate at least what's on offer, even if you are content with your lot. You must constantly seek to expand your horizons, to improve your working skills and to gain perspective.

Jupiter brings you some lucky communications and correspondence throughout 2009, and the important transition of this planet from Capricorn to Aquarius shows that there will be a shift from any financial complacency to a proactive approach to understanding how to maximise your resources. Your interest in superannuation, banking and other forms of investment are best tackled throughout March, April and May. This will also tie in with your work and a drive to achieve a better position around May. If you're not able to secure extra cash in hand, don't forget to try bargaining with a few lurks and perks such as additional superannuation payments, or lease payments on a car if you can wangle it. Your charm will work wonders throughout May and June, so don't underestimate what you can achieve in your professional life.

For Cancerians who are not actively in the workforce as such, but who are home-makers and executing their duties behind the scenes, 2009 can still be an excellent year in which they can forge ahead. Use your skills and your social network to assist you in earning more money in July. The combination of Mars and Venus gives you enough drive to pull all the factors together to make a modest success for yourself.

July through until September is also great for correspondence and clearing up any contractual loose ends. August in particular requires you to be a little more diligent about how you word your ideas. Any sloppiness on your part could mean a lost opportunity or, worse still, confusion, leading to disputes. Read all the fine print in contracts and, of course, if you have any doubts, run them by a seasoned professional for a second opinion.

Throughout October there are some important developments in the arena of your property and real estate zone. Some Cancerians could feel more comfortable shifting their work activities to the home arena. Or, if you've been working at home, you may choose to move your business to another location and this could bring better understanding of what you want in your employment.

This is further highlighted by the fact that the full Moon on the 4th occurs in your professional sphere with the new Moon of the 18th in your domestic region. Around these times you'll be feeling even more stimulated, excited and passionate about the work that you're doing.

Be careful not to let disputes over money and material resources interfere with smooth working relationships in November. Mars is notorious for this sort of thing when it triggers your financial reactions. In some cases it allows for wasteful expenditure, so you'll need to be more resourceful and think long-term rather than simply gratifying yourself in the moment. Those shopping sprees need to be restrained for a few weeks until this influence passes. Furthermore, the Sun and Mercury will prod you to be more speculative, which can result in bad gambling episodes in which nothing much is achieved; in fact, you may lose. It's essential for you to listen to the advice that is given to you during the closing month of the year because this will help solidify your financial security and future.

On the 16th December the new Moon in your sixth zone of work and daily routine is important. This occurs just before Christmas and emphasises the importance of being clear on your schedule and the events that you will need to address and be part of in the last few weeks of 2009. Spend time alone working out your time and prioritising those people who need you instead of those who simply want you. This will save you many problems and, rather than acting on a knee jerk reaction, you'll be on top of the entire set of social and business affairs without too much stress.

This also indicates that your health and wellbeing may need a revision so that you can optimise your life force and enjoy Christmas with greater vim and vigour.

Karma, luck and meditation

You have a brief window of opportunity to make the most of what you can through lucky partnerships in the early part of January. If you're inattentive, you may miss a vital introduction or chance to further your own luck and good fortune. Pay strict attention to the people you meet and under no circumstances should you judge a book by its cover. This is important as someone you'll be introduced to in January may not look or seem at all important enough, wealthy enough or connected enough to help give you the lucky break that can bring you some tremendously fortunate karma. They say that all that glitters is not gold, but the reverse is also sometimes true as well.

There are some other lucky breaks available to you from February to June due to the movement of Venus in your professional sector. Your inner glow and spiritual energies will attract plenty of good karma and opportunities for you then. In May the Moon and one of the karmic points of the zodiac tell me that you may be particularly susceptible to strong psychic vibrations. Remain open to your feelings and you will gain some strategic advantage.

Luck in friendships is highlighted throughout June and July. Some of these friendships may be fleeting and the experience you gain from them will be of only short-term value. Some people are simply catalysts to help you grow, and in August and September you'll be able to think deeply over what you've learned for the last part of the year and apply this to further your chances of success.

I see some karmic connections with brothers and sisters in October and November. Re-establishing your relationships can also be emotionally settling and will then free up much of your energy for the task of achieving greater successes in 2009 and beyond.

2009:
Month by Month
Predictions

If you begin to understand what you are without trying to change it, then what you are undergoing is a transformation.

—J. Krishnamurti

Highlights of the month

January is a sizzling time for you romantically with Venus and Neptune bringing out your fantasy and sexual imagination. You'll be deep in your feelings and active in your social and romantic life this month. Mars, the Sun, Jupiter, Mercury and the intense and revolutionary Pluto push you into deep waters emotionally.

Between the 3rd and 7th your attention will be drawn towards actively engaging with friends and enjoying the company of many diverse people. You'll need to use good judgement in determining which people you meet are going to offer you stable and honest relationships.

Up until the 15th, whether you like it or not, you'll be forced to probe a little more deeply into the meaning of life, sexuality and relationships. For some esoteric Cancerians, there will be a tinge of spiritual insight connected to their relationships.

There is a strong spirit of co-operation in your professional arena. You'll have excessive amounts of energy and actively want to join with others and share your ideas for the benefit of the team. Take care not to push your ideas too strongly because some elements of your career life may not be as cordial as you would like them to be. There may also be an unconscious desire to climb the ladder of success both socially and career wise, and this could lead you to walking a tightrope in terms of your professional and domestic/family responsibilities.

With Jupiter entering the eighth zone of shared resources and money, this is also a lucky time for combining investments and new businesses.

Be careful after the 23rd, however, as Mars's presence in your partnership zone could also indicate a bumpy road in this area of business, especially if you team up with people who are hard-nosed and irritable, especially Aries and Scorpio folk.

You want to do things in a big way and growth is certainly on the cards in the first part of 2009. You also wish to enhance your spiritual perspective this year and Jupiter is likely to do that for you due to its placement in the house of the zone of transformations.

The solar eclipse on the 26th January also adds weight to your spiritual interest and evolution in January. Your mind will soar to new heights and this is certainly a period where turning over a new leaf and bringing out the best in your character is more than likely.

Romance and friendship

This is a month in which your words flow, Cancer, and on the 1st when Mercury and Jupiter make contact, your thinking processes will be clear and your ideas will make an impact on your friends. Integrity, honesty and closeness in similarity of ideals seem to be the key words in this first part of the month.

On the 2nd, your mind is penetrating and you will be trying to ferret out solutions to some of your romantic problems; however, you may well find out a few facts that you hadn't bargained for.

Between the 3rd and the 6th your popularity is strong and you have contact with travellers, strangers or friends who may be coming and going. This is a celebratory time.

Sorting out some of your financial similarities and differences between the 6th and the 10th will be important if you are going to develop a deeper relationship with loved ones but get all the facts and figures correct first.

On the 12th and 13th you're more serious than usual but this will work to your advantage. Unfortunately people don't tend to take humour as a mark of commitment or responsibility and so a straighter face will get others onside in your discussions.

On the 19th, Mercury again makes contact with Jupiter and so something you've said may come back to haunt you. Make sure that you keep records of times, dates and specific discussions for reference material if people question your motives or your integrity.

An agreement is reached around the 21st and 22nd that is mutually beneficial to all parties concerned. If you've been in a long-term relationship, this transit indicates a solidification of your commitment to each other.

On the 22nd you may have doubt about your self-worth. Try to look at the better qualities in your character rather than dwelling on your shortcomings.

Between the 24th and the 28th your passions are strong and you are likely to experience many moments of intimacy and pleasure. On the 26th, the solar eclipse highlights this fact.

Work and money

The full Moon occurs on the 11th in your finance sector and shows that your mind is preoccupied with issues of income and expenditure. From the 2nd, when Mercury enters your zone of shared resources, your focus will primarily be on clearing debts and ensuring there's enough money to cover your expected expenses. It's wise to do this early in the year.

After the 18th, small wins are sweet. If you're going to a club, playing bingo, the pokies or even betting on a horse, it could be your lucky day.

Professional circumstances are a little harrowing after the 22nd. Miscommunications could cost you time as you try to explain and justify your words and actions. Double-check your correspondence before pressing the send button. You can make a lasting impression on others when the Sun and Jupiter join on the 24th. If you have a bright idea, share it. This is the stuff that dreams are made of; people will take you seriously and offer you a few unexpected opportunities. This is also favourable for acquiring investors' money if you are looking to do a business deal.

Independently employed Cancerians are lucky on the 27th, 28th and 29th when the planets favour communications, business dealings and contractual arrangements.

Destiny dates

Positive: 1, 2, 3, 4, 5, 11, 15, 18, 21, 24, 25, 26, 27, 28, 29

Negative: 8, 9, 10, 19

Mixed: 6, 7, 12, 13, 22, 23

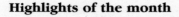

Highlights of the month

The first week of February is likely to be hectic and fraught with some professional challenges. The presence of Mars means you're likely to have a high energy level and drive to get things done; but try to curb any impulsive behaviour. In particular, you may be a little too headstrong around the 4th.

An important transit of Saturn and Uranus occurs around the 5th and this shows that your restless spirit needs to break free of any imposed constraints. Frustration is likely if you're fed up with dancing to another person's tune and you will decide to make some important changes.

The period of the 6th to the 15th is important because the lunar eclipse takes place in your zone of finances. You may feel like 'the odd man out' when there is a difference of opinion in the family over how money is spent or saved. You'll recognise that mostly this is an internal struggle of yours and for you alone to resolve.

Good relationships with perhaps a whole new group of people could happen after the 14th. You could meet someone whom you feel you've known from some other time, possibly a karmic connection? Your interest in travel and higher education could be triggered by this individual and inspire you to a much higher standard of life.

You'll have a great deal of confidence around the 18th and your competitive nature, coupled with the spirit of enterprise, can bring you further good luck or resolution in areas where your money or material resources are pooled. If on the home front you've had continuing problems of a financial nature, someone may finally agree to your way of seeing things.

When the Sun enters the ninth house after the 19th, the travel bug will bite even stronger and if you have the resources to do it now, a journey would be perfect.

Your personal power is lifted to great heights by the last few days of the month due to the Sun casting its beneficial rays on you, Cancer. You will feel important, with more physical and emotional strength than usual, and making an impact on others won't seem quite as difficult.

If you wish to make an impression on employers or others who can help you move forward with your ambitions, this will be a good time to make the approach.

Romance and friendship

You can find a great deal of satisfaction by engaging in many activities with family, partying with friends, and being with others of like-mind. The full Moon on the 9th is particularly encouraging and brings your feelings to the surface.

Between the 1st and the 10th of the lunar eclipse, you will be restless and hungry for new experiences. Around the 8th an old friend could resurface, triggering many nostalgic and senti-mental feelings. Catching up on old times and sharing similar experiences will be eye opening.

On the 12th and 13th, you are particularly idealistic. You want your family life to be the best it can. Although you may feel carefree, there could be some confusion over your or another family member's role in the group dynamic. Talking about it could clear up any misunderstandings.

On the 14th you have a lot of zest and enthusiasm; but you need to be careful not to overdo things because it could put someone offside as you try to find enough time for both work and pleasure.

Unusual meetings around the 16th are exciting and bring you in touch with people who are a little outside your normal day-to-day contacts. You could meet a foreigner or someone exotic who stokes your fire intellectually and probably physically, too.

The new Moon on the 25th, along with other planetary influences, hints at an opportunity for you to travel, perhaps by reconnecting with friends or fulfilling one of your short-term desires or goals.

By the 28th you feel festive and want a good time with friends. This is the perfect time to forge new alliances over the Internet through e-mails. Or, if you don't use computers, you could commence a pen pal friendship.

In the last few days of the month the Sun creates a very favourable set of vibrations making you more popular than ever.

Work and money

Around the 2nd you will realise that some of your old systems of work and money have probably worked more efficiently for you than any newer approach. Remember the old saying 'If it ain't broke, don't fix it'?

On the 5th, your frame of mind is 'Out with the old and in with the new', and this can be about a job or possibly some attitudes you've held closely for a long time. These challenges will help you to grow and improve your work skills.

Excellent opportunities on the 14th and 15th to forge fresh business contacts will open up new markets and generally make a good impression on others. Between the 16th and the 17th, discussions with your financial advisers, lawyers and other people involved in your future financial security will yield good results. Don't let the fear of looking stupid stop you from raising concerning issues.

Research and education is important between the 18th and 19th. Arm yourself with the facts before going into work meetings because with them you can achieve success in some minor battle.

On the 20th, you may have to adjust your attire in an approach to making a presentation. You could lose some ground if you insist on resisting change.

You're intense on the 21st, with the Sun and Pluto indicating the need for you to lighten up a little. Tact and diplomacy will bring better results than beating people about the head with your point of view.

Destiny dates

Positive: 1, 2, 3, 8, 19, 25, 28

Negative: 21

Mixed: 4, 5, 6, 7, 8, 9, 10, 11, 12, 13, 14, 15, 16, 17, 20

Highlights of the month

You'll be using your mind and imagination much more this month and, with Mercury forming good aspects to the upper part of your horoscope, it's time to open the lines of communication and clearly express your ideas to the world. Others are possibly not quite as psychic or as intuitive and you don't want to leave them second-guessing what's on your mind. Your ideas will not only be fun but productive and commercially viable.

The period of the 15th to the 17th is exciting and adventurous for you. Don't turn your back on an idea, even if at first it seems a little too wild for your tastes. You could find yourself in the company of brazen or at least cheeky people who invite you to try something different. This might scare you a little, particularly if you're a homebody type of Cancerian. Still, nothing ventured, nothing gained.

There will be time for a little more focus and concentration around the 19th when Mercury, the ruler of your thinking and communication, enters into relationship with Saturn. Don't think too hard, though, because valuable time may be wasted and then you'll be playing catch-up to get yourself organised again. You should expect a few delays but this doesn't necessarily mean the deal or the situation is lost. Try to remain buoyant and optimistic under all circumstances.

This time of the year is usually excellent for Cancerians in their choice of work. The Sun is powerful, as is the new Moon on the 26th, and your social status and professional standing can reach a pinnacle. You will be well received and may even be fortunate enough to take on a new and better-paying role.

Your social life will be buzzing at this time during the Mercury and Uranus interplay. It's under these transits that an invitation to an unusual event will stimulate your thinking, and possibly even your palate, if the dinner is held in a culturally unusual environment.

You could feel very affectionate in the last couple of days of March when the Sun and Venus combine their energies and produce wonderful feelings of exhilaration for you. You can rekindle your affection for the ones you love and, if you're not yet attached to anyone, you may find yourself falling head over heels in love with someone to whom you're introduced.

Romance and friendship

Take off those rose-coloured glasses around the 5th, when Mercury conjoins with Neptune. If you make assumptions about how someone sees you, you will probably be wrong, so to ease your mind, ask your partner or lover how they feel about certain things.

Be careful after the 8th when Mars and Neptune conjoin in your zone of sexuality. You may be confused about how to express yourself and this can sometimes relate to alcohol, pharmaceuticals or drugs. It's best to remain sober if you are trying to convey just how you feel to the person you love or have feelings for.

On the 9th your mind is penetrating and you can see into the motives of others. You won't be surprised to learn that someone is pulling your leg and you'll see straight through their ruse.

The period of the 11th until the 15th is excellent for all manner of ways to raise your social profile. Others will want to share in your fun and you may need a social secretary to keep up with the many offers that will be coming your way! Try not to overdo it, though, as there's always a downside to living too hard and too fast.

Your reputation continues to grow, particularly after the 26th when Mercury moves into the upper part of your horoscope. This is a chance to prove that you are not just a physical being but have considerable mental or intellectual substance as well. You will be respected for putting forward your opinions.

If you are not yet in love, something you say or do around the 28th could attract just the right person into your life. Could this be your soulmate? You will certainly be in contact with some very, very interesting people.

Your physical drive and competitiveness is strong on the 29th and 30th, but this could come at a cost. You're likely to be pushing others beyond their limits and may even be argumentative. Try to temper your opinions and people will be more amenable to your perspective.

With the Sun and Mercury combination occurring on the 31st, it's a fine end to the month and again you can make your mark among your peers. Don't be afraid to extend your social network by getting as many business cards and telephone numbers as possible.

Work and money

It's one of the finest times of the year to assert yourself in your professional or work activities. Venus highlights this fact and makes you popular, particularly between the 3rd and the 6th when your charm will work wonders.

Several social events linked to your work will not only further your career but can also act as a catalyst for developing new friendships and social alliances. By the 9th there could be some issues related to agreements, travel arrangements or scheduling. This is also a cycle in which confusion and slow thought processes could cause you to miss vital facts regarding contractual obligations.

Between the 16th and the 18th, expect abrupt changes on the work scene. Some new characters may not make you feel all that comfortable.

Excellent omens in the heavens are evident around the new Moon of the 26th and this can give you a fresh lease of life in your work. This leads to additional income after the 28th by way of a pay rise or even some better than expected commissions.

Destiny dates

Positive: 3, 4, 6, 11, 12, 13, 14, 15, 26, 28, 31

Negative: 8, 9, 18, 19, 29, 30

Mixed: 5, 16, 17

Highlights of the month

You might feel more like the Gemini twins this month as your mind is divided between two courses of action. The Sun creates some challenging energies for you as your constructive efforts meet with some resistance. These tensions will become increasingly annoying, particularly up until the 5th when Mars and Saturn compromise your relationships through heavy, deadlocked discussions.

The full Moon on the 9th occurs in your zone of domesticity. Although this tends to bring considerable focus emotionally to your relationship with loved ones, you'll also be challenged by authority figures who want more from you than you're prepared to give.

By the 10th, when Mercury enters your eleventh zone of fulfilment, you may be able to come to some understanding and, on the 15th, some revolutionary information can either resolve your emotional differences once and for all, or take the conflict to an even more intense level. Your communication skills will certainly be tested during this cycle.

You can be more conscientious about your work objectives due to the excellent placement of the Sun, Venus and Mercury in your horoscope this month, but it will be against a backdrop of emotional tensions you need to work through.

74

When the Sun enters your eleventh zone of friendships around the 20th, there may be an opportunity for you to connect with other like-minded people, who will help you see an alternative way of dealing with your issues. The new Moon on the 25th brings forth a new friend or ally who has considerable wisdom and this could be the start of a great new friendship.

Venus conjoining with Mars is also excellent and it shows that your passions are strong and healthy, bringing with it ample opportunity to explore your independence and deeper desires for sexual and physical pleasure. I only hope that if you're in a long-term relationship you'll have the opportunity to do so without upsetting the applecart too much.

Your personal power and magnetism is particularly strong between the 23rd and 30th when the Sun creates a very powerful aspect with Pluto. You should be sexually accepted and, if you've been holding back from letting the world know how you really feel about things, this could be an important turning point, not just in 2009 but also for your life as a whole.

Romance and friendship

The Moon commences its track in the quieter zone of your horoscope on the 1st but quickly moves to energise you emotionally. Possessiveness, jealousy and other forms of emotional negativity mustn't be allowed to mar an otherwise good day.

On the 4th your passionate desires could reach a fever pitch and, if your partner is not quite as intense as you, this could cause some setbacks in your personal relationships. It will be easy to project your feelings of inadequacy onto others and imagine that they're trying to make a move on your partner.

The sextile aspect from the Sun to Jupiter on the 11th is a magnificent, generous and abundant combination, which signifies a new phase of luck and growth, materially and spiritually. Why not just revel in the feeling and let this carry you along for a while?

Enjoy your own company and, believe it or not, the universe will attract the right people to you at just the right time.

Your creative pursuits should be actively fostered between the 16th and the 20th. Sharing similar interests and hobbies with a group of friends or work colleagues will bring you immense satisfaction.

This could result in some passionate interplay by the 22nd when Venus and Mars combine their sexy influences on your horoscope. You might even choose to be a little bit different and to step outside your traditional role in this sense. This has much to do with the proximity of Uranus in the zone of your ethics and philosophical beliefs.

Don't overdo things on the 27th, because you have a tendency to push your physical being beyond its limits. Partying hard, excessive drinking or even taking on too much exercise if you haven't been in the loop for a while, could do more harm than good.

Work and money

This month your professional aptitude will be tested and the adage that says 'Until you make it, fake it' may not work. You may be asked to prove what you are saying and therefore should only agree to tasks you feel absolutely confident about.

Between the 3rd and the 5th additional financial responsibilities will find you hot under the collar but unable to do much about it. The abrasive Mars and Saturn aspect means that you will feel like one foot is on the brake and one is on the accelerator both at the same time! Result: lots of smoke but going nowhere.

You must get through this and up until the full Moon on the 9th these difficulties may cause you a few sleepless nights and unwanted aggravation. However, thereafter I see a return to a more peaceful state of mind. You are motivated to get things done and will have a chance to assume a leadership role in this cycle. Just be careful, though, that you don't step into the shoes of a big person as you may not be able to fill them adequately.

Excessive amounts of work between the 22nd and the 26th means you may need some time out to recuperate. Don't punish yourself if you feel the going is getting a little tough. Overall this is a productive month but one in which you must manage your emotional and internal energies carefully.

Destiny dates

Positive: 10, 11, 15, 16, 17, 18, 19, 20, 28, 29, 30

Negative: 1, 3, 4, 5, 9

Mixed: 22, 23, 24, 25, 26, 27

Highlights of the month

The magical influence of Venus and Mars continues to bewitch you, reflecting this in your relationships by attracting many new friends and workplace opportunities. You'll feel many new energies emerging in yourself and this can be a delicate balancing act for you to explore and express how you feel while at the same time meeting your responsibilities head on.

The full Moon on the 9th is an important indicator of just how much you wish to enjoy life in May. After the difficult and frustrating challenges of Mars and Saturn in April, you'll be breathing a sigh of relief and simply wanting to have some fun and entertainment. Between the 9th and 12th you can do so, with the exception of the 11th, when you may have a few niggling health issues that need to be addressed.

On the 17th you'll be particularly progressive in your thinking and will be drawn to an unusual person. Keep an open mind if you wish to join forces with someone like this, either socially or professionally; but remember, what at first seems attractive and exciting may later have its drawbacks.

The Sun and Neptune are particularly prone to creating confusion and can mess with your ability to make clear financial decisions. You're probably going to be quite impressionable and must therefore not hand over money just because an idea sounds great. Keep listening, but say little.

After the quietening new Moon of the 24th your confidence builds to the 27th, but this will make you feel like a turtle, pulling your head in and re-evaluating some of your thoughts and feelings, especially if you're a parent. Some of the younger people in your life may need more attention. This is the time for you to take a good hard look at your relationship with them; at yourself as a role model, and to perhaps change some of the ways you deal with them.

You'll be positive and successful in addressing these issues so I don't see this as being a problem. The important association of Jupiter and Neptune will have a powerful influence on you over the coming few weeks and will be explained in the next chapter in your forecast for June.

Romance and friendship

The Sun forms a powerful aspect to your seventh zone of partnerships and relationships. You may be extending your hand in friendship only to find the other person is self-absorbed and working through some strange and unexpressed issues. It's best to leave them to their own devices.

There may be certain personal issues affecting your own mental stability between the 2nd and the 4th. You, being the type of person who may not want to burden others, might get to the bottom of these issues so that you can improve your relationships as a result.

The 7th, 8th and the full Moon of the 9th are wonderful for entertainment and joining in cultural or creative activities. A friend or lover will catch you off guard by being particularly creative and amorous towards you, which will cause you embarrassment in your group.

Mercury prods you to make contact with people you've ignored around the 13th and 14th. Social obligations dictate that you give and take and, if you've been self-absorbed or just too busy with family responsibilities, make the effort and give that friend or lover a call.

You might feel obliged to spend excessive amounts of time and money on someone to prove your friendship and love, especially after the 16th. It's not what you give or how much it's worth but the spirit in which you do it. If you happen to be in a group who measures your worth by what you have or how much money you are prepared to share then it may be time to rethink those associations, don't you think?

You might also find yourself in a confusing state of affairs between the 21st and the 23rd when you're invited to a function that is completely at odds with your social, cultural or financial means. Rather than feel uncomfortable about the whole event it might be best to decline the offer.

You feel revived and energetic on the 27th and the 28th when Mars and Jupiter inspire you with big new plans. You are able to give and receive equally and feel as though your friendships are now on a more even keel.

Work and money

If your passion for work duties has dimmed somewhat this won't leave you feeling refreshed and ready to tackle your job. Mars and Venus are strong in the upper part of your horoscope and it could be that some of the players in your working life have also changed, giving you a better feeling of camaraderie and friendship.

On the 10th and 11th you can feel focused and clear on your objectives. A dynamic approach to your duties creates a perfect environment for you and everyone around you, thus work can seem more fun and less monotonous.

On the 15th you'll find it difficult separating truth from fiction, so don't rely on what others tell you. It's going to take extra time to find the truth but it's better to be correct than later finding yourself with egg on your face.

Around the 19th and 20th romance with a new and attractive employee can blossom in the workplace, but be careful; it's wise not to mix business with pleasure.

You have an opportunity after the new Moon of the 24th to travel for work and maybe to spend some time away at a conference or even sourcing new business for your company.

Destiny dates

Positive: 8, 9, 10, 11, 12, 17, 24, 25, 26, 27, 28

Negative: 11, 16, 19, 20, 21, 22, 23

Mixed: 2, 3, 4, 13, 14

Highlights of the month

The eighth zone of your horoscope is one of those astrological areas that is difficult to discuss. This is because at first glance it relates to money, wills, inheritances and death, etcetera; but at a deeper and more philosophical level it involves transformation of a spiritual nature for you in 2009.

Between the 1st and the 7th, you may question your values, your religious views and ethics and ask yourself whether or not these things have served you well enough to date. This is a period of exploration and examination of the practical values of these issues.

The full Moon on the 7th hints at you wanting to change your day-to-day routine, possibly even the nature of your work, especially if feeling unfulfilled in your role.

For mothers who are at home with kids, it could be time for you to seek outside work and reconnect with a wider circle of people. For already working Cancers, you might want a role that is more than a means to an end, possibly providing a useful service to the community.

Tapping into the meaning of life and how this relates to your actions on a daily basis will be one of the important questions you'll be seeking answers to throughout June.

You're advised not to travel in the first part of the month because the Moon and Saturn can cause you to overlook important elements of the journey. The Moon in Uranus also causes you to be highly strung and, particularly between the 16th and 22nd, your knee jerk reactions to situations might cause you to overlook important facts and figures. Friends and strangers alike will be overwhelmed by your magnetic and electric aura this month.

Venus continues to chase Mars up until the 21st when your common interests with a friend can bring you either love or a new artistic direction. Expressing yourself through the creative arts, cooking or musical outlets brings much happiness to you during this phase.

Whereas earlier the problems between Mars and Saturn challenge you, in the last week of the month you're able to harness the energy of these two planets. You can get a lot done and a sense of accomplishment will make June a productive month overall.

Romance and friendship

Who's with you and who's against you? Mars sneaks into your zone of friendships and it may be troublesome for your social activities this month. Someone you know may be demanding so much more than you feel is fair around the 3rd, so you need to speak up and draw the line. This could be the ending of the friendship and a new chapter in your life when you realise you don't need the aggravation that this person gives you.

However, you'll be surprised that, by the full Moon of the 7th and more likely on the 8th, your firm stand on how you wish to be treated will be met with considerably more respect. It's quite likely in my prediction that a relationship seemingly at its end will in fact turn around so it can be renewed rather than relinquished.

We all like surprises and it's likely that between the 9th and 14th a sequence of events will make life much more interesting. It is also likely you will be the recipient of a gift or accolade and this could be to do with community work or group activities in which you're involved. It could be that you are nominated to take the leading role or head up a committee on a project that will excite and inspire you to do better.

The planets will provide you wonderful business and financial opportunities on the 18th, 21st and 22nd. All manner of interesting connections can be made at this time and, although you don't want to be seen as a user, keep the names of a few of these people you meet in your back pocket for future reference. I'm almost certain that someone you meet at this time will be a source of valuable information or possibly introduce you to someone who can make things happen for you on a professional level at a later date.

Karmic influences are strong around the 28th and I see some further resolution to a family conflict that may have been longstanding. Bury the hatchet now and enjoy simple, straightforward relations with relatives.

Work and money

With the dual planet Mercury in the zone of profits between the 1st and 3rd, some Cancers may toy with the idea of earning an additional income from a secondary source such as a home hobby.

Any speculating you do is powerful and profitable on the 3rd and 4th, but get your facts right before throwing your hard-earned money at the stock market. With the Moon in opposition in Mercury, resist impulsive investing and spend time getting to know your subject.

On the 8th, 9th, 12th and 14th allocate some time to researching these issues and, even if you have to pay someone for their advice, my strong recommendation is to do so.

If you have to spend your own money for a course or seminar to improve your professional life, treat it as an investment between the 15th and 17th. It may be an ideal way for you to step up to a new level that offers you potentially higher income.

Generally, when the Sun is in your zone of privacy, you'll get much more done on your own without mixing too much with others. You can collect your energies and, like a magnifying glass focusing the rays of the Sun, you too can beam the forces of your attention to achieve a great deal in June.

Destiny dates

Positive: 8, 9, 10, 11, 12, 13, 14, 28

Negative: 16, 17, 18, 19, 20

Mixed: 1, 2, 3, 4, 5, 6, 7, 21, 22

Highlights of the month

We wish people many happy returns around their birthday and this is because your Sun is returning to its birth position. For you, Cancer, July is indeed the time when the Sun brings its warm and ennobling energy to your Sun sign and lifts your spirits, energising you.

On the 2nd and the 3rd, you'll be intense and want results without any interference from others; however, you'll be prepared to put many of your resources into an idea you believe in, and are prepared to go it alone if necessary.

Great communications and letters of interest after the 3rd further encourage you in your path. You'll receive good news by the 6th or the full Moon of the 7th, so patiently wait for that important response.

A lunar eclipse on the 7th has an important story to tell and reveals some of the hidden side of your relationship and family history. Everyone has a past and you mustn't be too judgemental when learning the truth, even if it's unpalatable.

A slower pace is likely from the 12th when Mars enters the introverted zone of your horoscope and also makes contact with your karmic planets. You may be seeking self-regeneration through connecting with your own inner self and feel perfectly fine about it, even if your friends don't.

Charitable work is likely in this phase and you may be inspired by a story you read or something you see on television that causes you to help others who are less fortunate than yourself.

Between the 18th and 22nd your commercial instincts are strong and you're able to sniff out a great deal. The new Moon on the 22nd brings renewed confidence in your skills as a negotiator and if you run an independent business or work in sales you could expect your profits to rise dramatically in the last few days of the month.

A solar eclipse occurs in your Sun sign on the 22nd as well. This is an important celestial event and can revolutionise your views of both yourself and the world around you. This year is shaping up to be an incredibly transformative one for you and if you use these energies wisely great success is likely now and into the future.

On the 29th, 30th and 31st, sudden unexpected meetings with someone could cause you to flirt with romantic danger. Be careful.

Romance and friendship

July is an intense month for you, not just because the Sun is returning to its birth position in your horoscope, but also because many aspects are forming in the heavens. On top of this there are two eclipses, both of which powerfully influence your relationships. This is a critical month in which you may have some important decisions to make over the future direction of your love life.

On the 6th and 7th, in particular, you must decide whether or not a relationship has now come full circle. Do you want to go around again, or has it run its course? If the story's over, it may be time to part ways.

However, as the Moon moves through the zone of transformation on the 8th and 9th, you may be able to see a whole new side to this person and perhaps contemplate more of a future with them.

Your thinking and communication is particularly clear and concise on the 12th. Witty, sarcastic and humorous scenarios could tire you as you want more substance in the way of your personal friendships.

You may decide to house-sit for someone, or just have a change of scenery around the 12th or 13th. A change is often as good as a holiday.

A new relationship or friendship could cool around the 22nd when Venus and Saturn suddenly throw up a difference in style, and this could leave you feeling quite flat for a few days. Family members and close friends might also be discouraging you from entertaining a new relationship with this sort of person. You'll have to mediate on this and use your own inner resources to get through the situation.

Better conditions apply around the 28th when you have a realisation about the true worth of a person or persons in your life. If you do see the situation clearly, make a firm decision to avoid problems on the 29th, 30th and 31st.

Work and money

The karmic planet, the south node, is slowly but surely exiting your finance sector. You will now feel confident that your attitudes to money, prudence and foresight have afforded you a much more secure future as a result.

Although you may have a few temporary debts on the 3rd or 4th, you can quickly regain financial ground by the 7th and be back on track by the 9th.

Pay the bills that arrive around the 11th because you may forget them and be playing catch-up down the track. Around the 12th and 13th a legal issue or bureaucratic bungle could leave you feeling exasperated.

On the 14th, with your letter writing skills, you'll resolve any problems with people who have not been open to your calls for help.

The solar eclipse on the 22nd makes you realise that you may be destined for some new type of work in life, but it's up to you to seek out opportunities.

The period of the 22nd and 23rd finds you are working overtime to make some extra money. Mercury being opposite to Jupiter on the 30th is problematic for your health; so for peace of mind, take the time to seek professional advice.

Destiny dates

Positive: 8, 9, 14, 18, 19, 20, 21, 23, 28

Negative: 2, 3, 4

Mixed: 6, 7, 11, 12, 13, 22, 29, 30, 31

Highlights of the month

It's not quite true to say that money is the root of all evil; rather, the love of money is the problem. This month highlights your focus on the material aspects of life with the Sun, Mercury and the new and full Moons bringing much energy and attention to your income and financial status.

On the 1st, Venus creates overall popular instances in your work and gives you the chance to shine in the public eye. If you're not prone to stepping out into the limelight, you'll find yourself just that little bit more attractive at home, with your family lavishing attention upon you.

You're likely to be the recipient of some good news around the 4th or 5th and this could be in the way of a gift or token of appreciation for some work you've done in the past. It's these small things that occur in our lives that can often have more of an impact on us than we care to think.

Although the good-looking and attractive power of Venus is welcomed by all of us, it too can sometimes create its own little dramas, which could be the case when it enters the opposition of Pluto. It's likely someone could become jealous of your new look or your heightened sexual prowess and might try to assert him- or herself on the matter of your independence and choice of friends. Speak your mind and don't allow territorial disputes to spoil an otherwise good relationship.

By the 10th the more harmonious vibrations of Venus are likely to be felt and the Moon in the upper part of your horoscope can give you a sense of accomplishment. All things beautiful will take centre stage for you and you'll be attractive to the world around you.

The aspect of Mars to Saturn again challenges you through its devitalising energies between the 11th and 15th. Try not to bottle up your feelings and, if you again meet with some resistance, your self-control needs to be exercised. Keep a smile on your face and don't allow these energies to ruin an otherwise fruitful month. 'Live and let live' is the best approach.

Excellent financial prospects are in store for you this month, with business deals proving profitable, especially after the 19th and 20th. Choose the right people to be involved with and work together by recognising one another's talents.

Romance and friendship

Venus enters your Sun sign from the 1st day of the month, bringing with it several weeks of charming and happy vibrations. In the first week or two you'll be quickly making appointments to change your hair colour, get your nails done, purchase that new suit if you're a guy and generally looking your best to impress the world with your ample bucket-loads of magnetism. It is also an excellent time in which to look forward to your relationships being happy and fulfilling on virtually every level.

A friend who has been distant will make greater efforts to show you how they feel and to be more supportive during this period, especially after the 3rd. On the 10th you may hear news from that person, even if they don't necessarily live locally. Be careful, though, as an approach by someone who's been out of the loop for a while is a veiled guise to request you help them in an underhanded way.

The Mars-square-Saturn influence on the 11th is a problem and indicates that for a few days you may not physically feel the best. You need to look after number one and perhaps refuse some invitations to get back to the strong Venus vibe that dominates August.

Travel, albeit short journeys perhaps for work, are also the flavour of the month and can trigger a lot of movement for you after the 23rd. I see you having a good time and making the most of it.

Between the 26th and the 27th, powerful energies influence your marital zone and this is an excellent time to commit to marriage or a long-term relationship. Some Cancerians in de facto relationships may finally realise it is time to move to the next level.

Work and money

The Sun can produce two very different types of effects moving through your zone of finance in August. One is a greater interest in directing your money into income-producing channels or, heaven forbid, burning a hole in your pocket. It is after all a fiery planet.

It's presently a strong business cycle for some Cancerians and new partnerships can be formed, especially after the 3rd. With Venus casting its favourable influence on all manner of relationships, including business, it's not likely you'll put a foot wrong. If you have stubborn, hard-headed business counterparts to deal with, your softer and more casual approach will be appreciated by them and could be the deciding factor in an otherwise difficult transaction.

A better cycle for you this month is between the 9th and 13th, at which point your industriousness will lead the way for others in your group. Your superiors will be particularly pleased with the way you're handling your work and duties.

Gossip on the 14th and 15th should be avoided like the plague. This could damage you in the eyes of your superiors and inadvertently set you up against others. Be diplomatic, a friend to all, and don't buy into this rumour-mongering.

The new Moon on the 20th is another omen that is fortuitous as far as your earnings are concerned. As I mentioned in July, this time of the year may be one in which a new source of income can be gained. You have the drive and the opportunities available to you between the 20th and 27th.

Destiny dates

Positive: 3, 4, 5, 9, 10, 19, 20, 21, 22, 24, 25, 26, 27

Negative: 14, 15

Mixed: 1, 11, 12, 13, 23

Highlights of the month

With the presence of Mars in your Sun sign, it would be an understatement to say you're all revved up, energetic and competitive, to say the least. You need to direct this physical aspect of your energy into productive channels and, if you do so, this can be a month in which enormous strides can be made. Due to a change in attitude, your willpower will be accentuated and there's nothing much you'll feel you can't do.

Take the lead between the 6th and 10th because others will be looking to you for leadership and direction. You're probably thinking to yourself: 'Dadhichi, what are you talking about? I am just a simple person who works a simple job without much influence on the world.' I say that your leadership can extend into the small things of life; for example, the quality of your work can have an impact on others even without you realising it. Perfect your work and put your creative energy into everything you do at this time. Not only will you produce great work but your mind will be still and you'll be empowered spiritually by this process.

There are a few tricky days between the 12th and 14th when the Moon enters into the conjunction with Mars. Keep focused on the work at hand and under no circumstances should you buy into gossip or third-party information. Keep to yourself and be attentive to the job at hand.

The new Moon on the 18th occurs at a time when the Sun is approaching a conjunction with Saturn. Additional responsibilities will be offered to you. Don't be afraid to take up the challenge because you will learn a great deal about yourself and others this month. By jumping into the deep end, you'll quickly learn how to swim.

By the 20th, when Venus brings its helpful vibrations to the picture, you'll be sitting pretty. It's also very likely that in the midst of these additional burdens of work or other people's issues, a new love can dawn. There'll be an urge to explore a new partnership or friendship and this will bring you much joy.

With Venus activating your third zone of communications, you'll enjoy a short trip or possibly even a vacation that you've planned for some time.

Venus and Pluto indicate a deepening and a sharing of your emotional self with someone. The act of opening your heart is the way to invite more love into your life and you'll quickly realise this in September.

Romance and friendship

Watch your step this month, Cancer, as Mars's presence in your Sun sign is not a welcome energy for your relationships. An irresistible force could hit an immovable object, particularly between the 6th and 12th. What you want and what your partner or spouse desire is the same, but you are coming at it from different angles. Be receptive to each other's needs and remember that satisfying another person means you ultimately satisfy yourself.

You're feeling physically motivated this month but also impatient and reactive to a large extent. On the 11th, be careful you don't injure yourself through rushing around carelessly.

Plan your day before hurrying out the door and you can avoid not just irritable moments, but potential physical harm.

You'll find yourself in the company of people who are mentally at odds with you on the 17th. You may be present at a luncheon or dinner only to please a friend but begrudge the fact that you had to attend at all.

Good news on the 19th or 20th can make you feel buoyant and more alive. A registered parcel or piece of information is likely and this can impact positively on your personal relationships and domestic activities.

Actively involving yourself with children between the 21st and 25th is also positive for you and, if you happen to be a parent, one of your children may be the recipient of some good fortune or success at a sporting event.

Venus continues to bring you good luck and inspire you between the 29th and 30th. Your personal aura is getting stronger.

Work and money

As I said in the previous segment, Mars can be disruptive, putting you at odds with people in your environment. Don't let Mars unsettle the sweet influence of Venus when it comes to discussions about money and agree to disagree. It's quite likely a conflict will arise, especially leading up to the 12th, when your approach to handling finances will be greatly different to that of your partner's.

A tricky situation at a work luncheon or casual outing could arise where a demand is made on you for more money than you feel you should pay. Get clarity before the event rather than floundering afterwards.

There's a desire to spend some money on your house by refurbishing or renovating. After the 18th, don't overextend yourself because you may simply be overcapitalising. However, if this is to have a bit more comfort and satisfaction or you are intending to work from home, go ahead.

Issues with a co-worker could arise from the 23rd to 28th when they dredge up some past error that you thought had been long dead and buried. This is probably more related to their insecurity than anything you are doing wrong in the present. Take it with a grain of salt.

Destiny dates

Positive: 19, 20, 21, 22, 29, 30

Negative: 12, 13, 14, 17, 18, 26, 27, 28

Mixed: 6, 7, 8, 9, 10, 11, 23, 24, 25

Highlights of the month

Once you overcome a few of the initial work obligations of the month up until the 5th, there'll be a shift in your attention to family and relatives. A few social gatherings between the 5th and 7th will be a welcome relief from some intense work demands. You'll want to participate in some active and humorous parties or events up until the 10th and I see you associating with large numbers of people during this phase.

Between the 11th and the 13th, you'll be surprised to receive information from someone from your past and could be reintroduced to them by a mutual friend.

Between the 15th and the 18th your energies are strongly directed to your home affairs. With the Sun also moving into the lower part of your horoscope you may have to wind down physically and emotionally, paying attention to this part of your life while the Sun is in this area of your horoscope.

Issues that have been swept under the rug for far too long may need to be addressed. It may be an uncomfortable task confronting someone you love with this matter, but it must happen. You may laugh, but it could be as mundane as a person leaving their socks in the hallway day after day and you having to pick up after them, which has left you with the unenviable task of having a quiet word in their ear. But once it is out of the way, you'll realise it wasn't such a big deal. Such is life.

Additional issues that may need to be addressed are those relating to money, debts and other expenses tied in with your family life. You may have an increased appetite for earning money but could find it is disappearing quicker than you had planned due to expenses elsewhere.

Someone may be less than frugal or responsible with money and if it's a partner you may again have to thrash things out to come to a mutual understanding. Don't avoid the issue because it could create bad blood between you.

Excellent contacts come your way from the 21st and this is an opportunity to cut a better deal for yourself. If you're in a situation where a workplace agreement is being offered you have a chance to alter the clauses of the contract so that the deal tilts in your favour.

Romance and friendship

Your friends and partners could surprise you this month by doing something completely out of the ordinary, and just when you thought they were a lost cause! This is at a critical time, too, because your own evolutionary spirit is strong this month and your sense of self is growing stronger, particularly after the 3rd. On the 5th you can take up their offer and party hard. Mars, Saturn and Uranus provide you with a rip-snorting good time.

With the destiny planets also influencing your personal relationships, it may be time for you to collect on your karmic rewards. Some of your past actions—the good deeds you've executed in your relationships—are starting to pay off.

On the 14th, Venus in sextile to Mars shows that your passionate involvement with friends and lovers is more than healthy and physical attractions continue to be strong. It's also a time of new romance for you.

Working with a loved one is possible after the 15th and you can harness both sets of talents to grow closer together as well as making a little money on the side.

You may meet someone with whom you can develop a great friendship at an art class or a music, dance or theatre environment. You may want to engage in some frivolous and fun activities between the 18th and 20th, but your inner voice tells you otherwise. There's no harm in having a little fun, but just know where to draw the line.

You're in tune with your loved one after the 23rd and, although you may feel a little restless in spirit, why not extend an invitation to them to join you in a little light, adventurous exploration around town? The 26th to the 30th brings you some flirtatious opportunities but be careful you don't hit on the wrong person.

Work and money

This month you need to define clearly your role at your work-place because, over time, additional workloads are subtly added until you reach breaking point when you realise you are doing way too much. By the 10th you may find yourself in a few undesirable skirmishes with your employer or other members of your household who really don't want to do their share of work. Assert yourself to gain what you want.

The 14th and 15th are light-hearted days during which you may not feel all that energised to do much work. It's not a bad idea to unwind and do your work in a more relaxed atmos-phere.

An opportunity to work from home around the 18th is a great idea and may trigger your interest in following a more independent line of work from here on in. If you're taking a lot of work home with you, you may need to create a better space in which to do so and be a little bit more productive.

On the 20th, because you are feeling on top of the world, you may be able to help others through their difficulties and create a few new allies along the way. You could be feeling somewhat listless on the 25th and 26th, and Neptune will lower your drive to anything ambitious. It's likely you'll feel comfortable just getting through the job rather than doing anything superhuman during the last few days of October.

Destiny dates

Positive: 6, 7, 11, 12, 13, 14, 15, 16, 17, 21, 23, 27, 28, 29, 30

Negative: 1, 2, 10, 25

Mixed: 3, 4, 18, 19, 20, 26

Highlights of the month

When Venus makes contact with Neptune, the higher ideals of love and emotional refinement come to the surface and make their presence felt in our lives. On the 3rd, these mystical and creative influences are felt in your home life and bring a touch of magic to your environment. This is where your own artistic ideals could find an outlet by way of refurbishing, redecorating and artistically enhancing your home and the environment in which you live. If you're a Cancerian who spends most of his or her time in the office, then you can apply your talents to making that a more comfortable area in which to work.

At this time, too, you may need to endure some workplace meetings, professional interactions and other corporate events that may be drab and not at all to your liking. For this reason, finding an artistic outlet will make this early part of November a little more palatable and enjoyable for you.

This is a time of comparisons with the lives of others, of appreciating just how lucky you are and I see the first week bringing you a level of appreciation for your own life and circumstances.

You mustn't be drawn into any tests of loyalty in your friendships after the 13th. You may not even realise that this is happening but, once you do, be careful of not overreacting and ruining a friendship.

The new Moon on the 16th again occupies your zone of love affairs, entertainment, speculation and sport. Between the 16th and 18th you may be compelled to take up a new sport or outdoor activity in which you can express yourself physically. Team sports are excellent under these transits and you may even be fortunate to meet someone of like-mind at an event where your friendship can develop into a more serious relationship.

Until the 22nd, get adequate rest and take a more consistent approach to your diet and lifestyle. Coupled with your interest in sport and becoming more active, this is a nice time of the year to raise your sense of wellbeing, not just physically but mentally and spiritually as well.

Your professional life can reach its peak by the 27th with the promise of a pay rise or additional cash in hand by the 29th.

Romance and friendship

If you maintain your convictions, you may not keep all your friends, but you'll still find your integrity intact. Speaking the truth around the 8th might not be too palatable for some of your friends but this will give you clarity and a sense that those who are genuinely supportive of you will accept what is said in the spirit of co-operation.

The entry of Saturn into your fourth zone of family life is very important and ushers in a new two-and-a-half-year cycle. Changes are on the agenda in your domestic world and this is the time to try to include your family members more. You may be feeling a little repressed emotionally, but I strongly recommend you control this and don't bottle up your feelings because this cycle can only make it a more daunting process to open up later.

Between the 12th and 19th, make that extra effort to connect with your parents or spouse to talk about the past and the meaning of life so that old issues are resolved to create a more conducive atmosphere at home.

Between the 19th and the 23rd you will feel an uplifting energy, which causes you to try harder in your married life. You will feel a stronger desire to succeed and a friend who may be experiencing similar issues will come to your rescue.

A few sensual escapades are on the cards around the 24th. This can be a fun time and also one in which you can explore your sexuality. Your interest in religious and philosophical matters can bring you closer to a friend around the 25th and you realise you have a common interest in some exotic philosophy or meditation theme.

The month closes on a great social note with the Moon bringing you in touch with a group of friends in an outdoor environment where it's just fun to hang out together, having a laugh.

Work and money

Remaining objective will be very important this month in all matters of finance, which will benefit everyone.

The 2nd, 3rd, 8th and 9th are important dates in which your discussions about money need to be tempered by respect and consideration to other parties. The truth is no doubt correct but can cut and hurt others.

Taking a more serious approach to real estate matters on the 12th is an excellent way for you to build your nest egg. Another family member may be interested in talking this matter through with you, with a view to a common financial interest. The new Moon on the 16th could yet again involve a younger member of the family or a child in some business transaction.

Listen carefully to some investment advice given to you between the 15th and 17th. If you're not the gambling type, managed trusts are a good alternative that should be investigated as your financial gains are positive and in surplus.

We all need to splurge sometimes and you can do so between the 19th and 22nd. There's no point in saving money if you can't have the odd enjoyment and self-indulgence. It's a nice way to finish off the month, particularly if you can bring some joy to others as a result.

Destiny dates

Positive: 12, 14, 15, 16, 17, 18, 19, 20, 21, 23, 24, 25, 27, 29

Negative: nil

Mixed: 2, 3, 8, 9, 13, 22

Highlights of the month

The full Moon on the 2nd suggests that you should take time out with the one you love, get away from it all and reconnect with each other without the distractions of day-to-day life. A brief escape together would be ideal, if you can manage it, especially with Christmas on your doorstep.

Stabilising your personal relationships will be high on your agenda in the last month of the year. Around the 4th, when Venus forms favourable aspects with Saturn, you'll be interested in making sure that your future emotional security is vouchsafed. Although you may feel that the passion in your life is somewhat lacking, you'll be quite happy to weigh this up against a more consistent emotional guarantee.

Around the 11th you can be decisive and you'll be able to handle whatever stress or problems are thrown at you.

If you have confrontational people to deal with on issues around the 15th, be prepared to postpone some of your engagements or activities to accommodate them. Avoid any nervousness and increase your vitamin and dietary supplements to handle the peak period coming at this time.

The Moon transits your career sector on Christmas Eve and this shows you may still have a few odd jobs and loose ends to tie up before finally enjoying the festive season.

Christmas Day is an interesting one for you in that the Sun conjoins Pluto in your seventh house, indicating power plays and emotional manipulations. There may be warring factions, members of the family who are opposed to each other, and it's up to you to get this information beforehand to avoid extreme tensions at the family gathering.

A quiet time in the last few days of December is shown by the aspect of Venus to Saturn, indicating a more traditional time for you this year. Choose the people you want as company and you'll be able to complete 2009 with the feeling that you've achieved what you set out to do.

When dealing with people in communication, try to keep a calm, balanced view of the situation rather than letting their statements rattle you. This, apart from keeping your body healthy, will also go a long way to providing you with fresh new insights into life and relationships thereby equipping you with some new spiritual ammunition for the coming year.

Romance and friendship

Although I'd like to say that the first part of December will be socially active, you may have far too much work on your plate to actually enjoy it, even if you do have a chance to spend some time with others. The 1st and 2nd are low-key days. The 3rd and 4th seem to be days in which you are reactive to friends. Don't be baited. They may only be joking with you.

Furthermore, the position of Venus in your zone of work and health makes you a little more serious about tying up loose ends before fully enjoying whatever the month of December offers you socially.

There are plenty of sizzling romantic opportunities available to you on the 5th and 6th; but is your mind otherwise preoccupied?

You could be a little aggressive going after your romantic choice of person around the 11th. This might have the opposite effect and scare them away! Use a little more finesse, even if you are actively seeking only some new friendships.

On the 15th, yet again you may find yourself at odds with community or social standards and values. You might be trying too hard to make a personal statement and this will work events against you. Such things as etiquette and personal attire are the main points that come to mind.

In the week leading up to Christmas you have a mixed bag of energies but by far the best is the Sun in sextile to Jupiter around the 15th, and the Sun in sextile to Neptune on the 16th. Venus in a third position to Mars on the 17th means that these three days are jam-packed with goodwill, fun and romantic and social opportunities.

It's nice to see that the entrance of the Sun into your public-relations zone occurs on the 22nd, just before Christmas, with Venus creating a wonderful influence on Christmas Day itself. This means Christmas 2009 should in fact bring you loads of fun and satisfaction.

If you can wisely select your guests, there shouldn't be any hiccups and the last week of December should be a festive one to round off the year beautifully.

Work and money

Watch your health around the 16th as you're likely to be quite highly strung and enervated. Your primary focus is on work this month, especially up until the 17th. The new Moon in Sagittarius with the Sun, Mercury and Venus all occupying your zone of employment attest to this fact.

Try not to overdo it as I know you'll be trying hard to cram as much of your work as possible into the last two weeks of the year. Try to delegate some of those duties to others if you're in a position to do so, even if you get a bit of flack.

A last-ditch attempt to save some money is probably not going to make too much of a difference to your overall savings for 2009, but you can put in place some new mechanism such as forced saving or a direct debit. which, if you implement now, will hold you in good stead as 2010 gets underway.

Just when you thought you had it all sewn up, some unexpected calls and 'bushfires' on the work front on the 22nd might throw you into a tailspin. These are short-lived so don't make too much out of the events and you'll be back on track by Christmas Eve. The Moon transiting your professional sector indicates a lot of fun and social activities associated with your co-workers. What a lovely end to the year! On the 26th and 27th, with the Moon in your social sphere, I can predict without doubt that your emotions will be lifted to a new high and a sense of satisfaction over your professional activities will prevail.

Destiny dates

Positive: 17, 26, 27

Negative: 1

Mixed: 3, 4, 5, 6, 11, 15, 16, 22

2009:
Astronumerology

Do not be too moral. You may cheat yourself out of much of life. So, aim above morality. Be not simply good; be good for something.

—David Henry Thoreau

The power behind your name

By adding the numbers of your name you can see which planet is ruling you. Each of the letters of the alphabet is assigned a number, which is tabled below. These numbers are ruled by the planets. This is according to the ancient Chaldean system of numerology and is very different to the Pythagorean system to which many refer.

Each number is assigned a planet:

AIQJY	=	1	**Sun**
BKR	=	2	**Moon**
CGLS	=	3	**Jupiter**
DMT	=	4	**Uranus**
EHNX	=	5	**Mercury**
UVW	=	6	**Venus**
OZ	=	7	**Neptune**
FP	=	8	**Saturn**
—	=	9	**Mars**

Notice that the number 9 is not allotted a letter because it is considered special. Once the numbers have been added you will see that a single planet rules your name and personal affairs. Many famous actors, writers and musicians change their names to attract the energy of a luckier planet. You can experiment with the table and try new names or add letters of your second name to see how that vibration suits you. It's a lot of fun!

Here is an example of how to find out the power of your name. If your name is John Smith, calculate the ruling planet by correlating each letter to a number in the table like this:

J O H N   S M I T H

1 7 5 5   3 4 1 4 5

Now add the numbers like this:

1 + 7 + 5 + 5 + 3 + 4 + 1 + 4 + 5 = 35

Then add 3 + 5 = 8

The ruling number of John Smith's name is 8, which is ruled by Saturn. Now study the name-number table to reveal the power of your name. The numbers 3 and 5 will also play a secondary role in John's character and destiny so in this case you would also study the effects of Jupiter and Mercury.

Name-number table

Your name number	Ruling planet	Your name characteristics
1	Sun	Charismatic personality. Great vitality and life force. Physically active and outgoing. Attracts good friends and individuals in powerful positions. Good government connections. Intelligent, dramatic, showy and successful. A loyal number for relationships.
2	Moon	Soft, emotional temperament. Changeable moods but psychic, intuitive senses. Imaginative nature and compassionate expression of feelings. Loves family, mother and home life. Night owl who probably needs more sleep.

Success with the public and/or the opposite sex.

| 3 | Jupiter | Outgoing, optimistic number with lucky overtones. Attracts opportunities without trying. Good sense of timing. Religious or spiritual aspirations. Can investigate the meaning of life. Loves to travel and explore the world and people. |

| 4 | Uranus | Explosive personality with many quirky aspects. Likes the untried and untested. Forward thinking, with many unusual friends. Gets bored easily so needs plenty of stimulating experiences. Innovative, technological and creative. Wilful and stubborn when wants to be. Unexpected events in life may be positive or negative. |

| 5 | Mercury | Quick-thinking mind with great powers of speech. Extremely active life; always on the go and lives on nervous energy. Youthful attitude and never grows old. Looks younger than actual age. Young friends and humorous disposition. Loves reading and writing. |

| 6 | Venus | Charming personality. Graceful and attractive character, who cherishes friends and social life. Musical or artistic interests. Good for money making as well as numerous love affairs. Career in |

the public eye is possible. Loves family but is often overly concerned by friends.

7	Neptune	Intuitive, spiritual and self-sacrificing nature. Easily duped by those who need help. Loves to dream of life's possibilities. Has healing powers. Dreams are revealing and prophetic. Loves the water and will have many journeys in life. Spiritual aspirations dominate worldly desires.
8	Saturn	Hard-working, focused individual with slow but certain success. Incredible concentration and self-sacrifice for a goal. Money orientated but generous when trust is gained. Professional but may be a hard taskmaster. Demands highest standards and needs to learn to enjoy life a little more.
9	Mars	Incredible physical drive and ambition. Sports and outdoor activities are keys to health. Combative and likes to work and play just as hard. Protective of family, friends and territory. Individual tastes in life but is also self-absorbed. Needs to listen to others' advice to gain greater success.

Your 2009 planetary ruler

Astrology and numerology are closely linked. Each planet rules over a number between 1 and 9. Both your name and your birth date are ruled by planetary energies. Here are the planets and their ruling numbers:

1 Sun; 2 Moon; 3 Jupiter; 4 Uranus; 5 Mercury; 6 Venus; 7 Neptune; 8 Saturn; 9 Mars

Simply add the numbers of your birth date and the year in question to find out which planet will control the coming year for you. Here is an example:

If you were born on 12 November, add the numerals 1 and 2 (12, your day of birth) and 1 and 1 (11, your month of birth) to the year in question, in this case 2009 (current year), like this:

Add $1 + 2 + 1 + 1 + 2 + 0 + 0 + 9 = 16$

Then add these numbers again: $1 + 6 = 7$

The planet ruling your individual karma for 2009 will be Neptune because this planet rules the number 7.

You can even take your ruling name number as shown on page 113 and add it to the year in question to throw more light on your coming personal affairs like this:

John Smith = 8

Year coming = 2009

Add $8 + 2 + 0 + 0 + 9 = 19$

Add $1 + 9 = 10$

Add $1 + 0 = 1$

This is the ruling year number using your name number as a basis. Therefore, study the Sun's (number 1) influence for 2009. Enjoy!

1 = Year of the Sun

Overview

The Sun is the brightest object in the heavens and rules number 1 and the sign of Leo. Because of this the coming year will bring you great success and popularity.

You'll be full of life and radiant vibrations and are more than ready to tackle your new nine-year cycle, which begins now. Any new projects you commence are likely to be successful.

Your health and vitality will be very strong and your stamina at its peak. Even if you happen to have the odd problem with your health, your recuperative power will be strong.

You have tremendous magnetism this year so social popularity won't be a problem for you. I see many new friends and lovers coming into your life. Expect loads of invitations to parties and fun-filled outings. Just don't take your health for granted as you're likely to burn the candle at both ends.

With success coming your way, don't let it go to your head. You must maintain humility, which will make you even more popular in the coming year.

Love and pleasure

This is an important cycle for renewing your love and connections with your family, particularly if you have children. The Sun is connected with the sign of Leo and therefore brings an increase in musical and theatrical activities. Entertainment and other creative hobbies will be high on your agenda and bring you a great sense of satisfaction.

Work

You won't have to make too much effort to be successful this year as the brightness of the Sun will draw opportunities to you. Changes in work are likely and if you have been concerned that opportunities are few and far between, 2009 will be different. You can expect some sort of promotion or an increase in income because your employers will take special note of your skills and service orientation.

Improving your luck

Leo is the ruler of number 1 and therefore, if you're born under this star sign, 2009 will be particularly lucky. For others, July and August, the months of Leo, will bring good fortune. The 1st, 8th, 15th and 22nd hours of Sundays especially will give you a unique sort of luck in any sort of competition or activities generally. Keep your eye out for those born under Leo as they may be able to contribute something to your life and may even have a karmic connection to you. This is a particularly important year for your destiny.

Your lucky numbers in this coming cycle are 1, 10, 19 and 28.

2 = Year of the Moon

Overview

There's nothing more soothing than the cool light of the full Moon on a clear night. The Moon is emotional and receptive and controls your destiny in 2009. If you're able to use the positive energies of the Moon, it will be a great year in which you can realign and improve your relationships, particularly with family members.

Making a commitment to becoming a better person and bringing your emotions under control will also dominate your thinking. Try not to let your emotions get the better of you throughout the coming year because you may be drawn into the changeable nature of these lunar vibrations as well. If you fail to keep control of your emotional life you'll later regret some of your actions. You must carefully blend thinking with feeling to arrive at the best results. Your luck throughout 2009 will certainly be determined by the state of your mind.

Because the Moon and the sign of Cancer rule the number 2 there is a certain amount of change to be expected this year. Keep your feelings steady and don't let your heart rule your head.

Love and pleasure

Your primary concern in 2009 will be your home and family life. You'll be keen to finally take on those renovations, or work on your garden. You may even think of buying a new home. You can at last carry out some of those plans and make your dreams come true. If you find yourself a little more temperamental than usual, do some extra meditation and spend time alone until you sort this out. You mustn't withhold your feelings from your partner as this will only create frustration.

Work

During 2009 your focus will be primarily on feelings and family; however, this doesn't mean you can't make great strides in your work as well. The Moon rules the general public and what you might find is that special opportunities and connections with the world at large present themselves to you. You could be working with large numbers of people.

If you're looking for a better work opportunity, try to focus your attention on women who can give you a hand. Use your intuition as it will be finely tuned this year. Work and career success depends upon your instincts.

Improving your luck

The sign of Cancer is your ruler this year and because the Moon rules Mondays, both this day of the week and the month of July are extremely lucky for you. The 1st, 8th, 15th and 22nd hours on Mondays will be very powerful. Pay special attention to the new and full Moon days throughout 2009.

The numbers 2, 11 and 29 are lucky for you.

3 = Year of Jupiter

Overview

The year 2009 will be a 3 year for you and, because of this, Jupiter and Sagittarius will dominate your affairs. This is very lucky and shows that you'll be motivated to broaden your horizons, gain more money and become extremely popular in your social circles. It looks like 2009 will be a fun-filled year with much excitement.

Jupiter and Sagittarius are generous to a fault and so likewise, your open-handedness will mark the year. You'll be friendly and helpful to all of those around you.

Pisces is also under the rulership of the number 3 and this brings out your spiritual and compassionate nature. You'll become a much better person, reducing your negative karma by increasing your self-awareness and spiritual feelings. You will want to share your luck with those you love.

Love and pleasure

Travel and seeking new adventures will be part and parcel of your romantic life this year. Travelling to distant lands and meeting unusual people will open your heart to fresh possibilities of romance.

You'll try novel and audacious things and will find yourself in a different circle of friends. Compromise will be important in making your existing relationships work. Talk about your feelings. If you are currently in a relationship you'll feel an upswing in your affection for your partner. This is a perfect opportunity to deepen your love for each other and take your relationship to a new level.

If you're not attached to someone just yet, there's good news for you. Great opportunities lie in store for you and a spiritual or karmic connection may be experienced in 2009.

Work

Great fortune can be expected through your working life in the next twelve months. Your friends and work colleagues will want to help you achieve your goals. Even your employers will be amenable to your requests for extra money or a better position within the organisation.

If you want to start a new job or possibly begin an independent line of business this is a great year to do it. Jupiter looks set to give you plenty of opportunities, success and a superior reputation.

Improving your luck

As long as you can keep a balanced view of things and not overdo anything, your luck will increase dramatically throughout 2009. The important thing is to remain grounded and not be too airy-fairy about your objectives. Be realistic about your talents and capabilities and don't brag about your skills or achievements. This will only invite envy from others.

Moderate your social life as well and don't drink or eat too much as this will slow your reflexes and lessen your chances for success.

You have plenty of spiritual insights this year so you should use them to their maximum. In the 1st, 8th, 15th and 24th hours of Thursdays you should use your intuition to enhance your luck, and the numbers 3, 12, 21 and 30 are also lucky for you. March and December are your lucky months but generally the whole year should go pretty smoothly for you.

4 = Year of Uranus

Overview

The electric and exciting planet of the zodiac Uranus and its sign of Aquarius rule your affairs throughout 2009. Dramatic events will surprise and at the same time unnerve you in your professional and personal life. So be prepared!

You'll be able to achieve many things this year and your dreams are likely to come true, but you mustn't be distracted or scattered with your energies. You'll be breaking through your own self-limitations and this will present challenges from your family and friends. You'll want to be independent and develop your spiritual powers and nothing will stop you.

Try to maintain discipline and an orderly lifestyle so you can make the most of these special energies this year. If unexpected things do happen, it's not a bad idea to have an alternative plan so you don't lose momentum.

Love and pleasure

You want something radical, something different in your relationships this year. It's quite likely that your love life will be feeling a little less than exciting so you'll take some important steps to change that. If your partner is as progressive as you'll be this year, then your relationship is likely to improve and fulfil both of you.

In your social life you will meet some very unusual people whom you'll feel are specially connected to you spiritually. You may want to ditch everything for the excitement and passion of a completely new relationship, but tread carefully as this may not work out exactly as you'd expected.

Work

Technology, computing and the Internet will play a larger role in your professional life this coming year. You'll have to move ahead with the times and learn new skills if you want to achieve success.

A hectic schedule is likely, so make sure your diary is with you at all times. Try to be more efficient and don't waste time.

New friends and alliances at work will help you achieve even greater success in the coming period. Becoming a team player will be even more important towards gaining satisfaction in your professional endeavours.

Improving your luck

Moving too quickly and impulsively will cause you problems on all fronts, so be a little more patient and think your decisions through more carefully. Social, romantic and professional opportunities will come to you but take a little time to investigate the ramifications of your actions.

The 1st, 8th, 15th and 20th hours of any Saturday are lucky, but love and luck are likely to cross your path when you least expect it. The numbers 4, 13, 22 and 31 are also lucky for you this year.

5 = Year of Mercury

Overview

The supreme planet of communication, Mercury, is your ruling planet throughout 2009. The number 5, which is connected to Mercury, will confer upon you success through your intellectual abilities.

Any form of writing or speaking will be improved and this will be, to a large extent, underpinning your success. Your imagination will be stimulated by this planet with many incredible new and exciting ideas coming to mind.

Mercury and the number 5 are considered somewhat indecisive. Be firm in your attitude and don't let too many ideas or opportunities distract and confuse you. By all means get as much information as you can to help you make the right decision.

I see you involved with money proposals, job applications, even contracts that need to be signed so remain clear-headed as much as possible.

Your business skills and clear and concise communication will be at the heart of your life in 2009.

Love and pleasure

Mercury, which rules the signs of Gemini and Virgo, will make your love life a little difficult due to its changeable nature. On the one hand you'll feel passionate and loving to your partner, yet on the other you will feel like giving it all up for the excitement of a new affair. Maintain the middle ground.

Also, try not to be too critical with your friends and family members. The influence of Virgo makes you prone to expecting much more from others than they're capable of giving. Control your sharp tongue and don't hurt people's feelings. Encouraging others is the better path, leading to more emotional satisfaction.

Work

Speed will dominate your professional life in 2009. You'll be flitting from one subject to another and taking on far more than you can handle. You'll need to make some serious changes in your routine to handle the avalanche of work that will come your way. You'll also be travelling with your work, but not necessarily overseas.

If you're in a job you enjoy then this year will give you additional successes. If not, it may be time to move on.

Improving your luck

Communication is the secret of attaining your desires in the coming twelve months. Keep focused on one idea rather than scattering your energies in all directions and your success will be speedier.

By looking after your health, sleeping well and exercising regularly, you'll build up your resilience and mental strength.

The 1st, 8th, 15th and 20th hours of Wednesday are lucky so it's best to schedule your meetings and other important social engagements during these times. The lucky numbers for Mercury are 5, 14, 23 and 32.

6 = Year of Venus

Overview

Because you're ruled by 6 this year, love is in the air! Venus, Taurus and Libra are well known for their affinity with romance, love, and even marriage. If ever you were going to meet a soulmate and feel comfortable in love, 2009 must surely be your year.

Taurus has a strong connection to money and practical affairs as well, so finances will also improve if you are diligent about work and security issues.

The important thing to keep in mind this year is that sharing love and making that important soul connection should be kept high on your agenda. This will be an enjoyable period in your life.

Love and pleasure

Romance is the key thing for you this year and your current relationships will become more fulfilling if you happen to be attached. For singles, a 6 year heralds an important meeting that eventually leads to marriage.

You'll also be interested in fashion, gifts, jewellery and all sorts of socialising. It's at one of these social engagements that you could meet the love of your life. Remain available!

Venus is one of the planets that has a tendency to overdo things, so be moderate in your eating and drinking. Try generally to maintain a modest lifestyle.

Work

You'll have a clearer insight into finances and your future security during a number 6 year. Whereas you may have had additional expenses and extra distractions previously, your mind will be more settled and capable of longer-term planning along these lines.

With the extra cash you might see this year, decorating your home or office will give you a special sort of satisfaction.

Social affairs and professional activities will be strongly linked. Any sort of work-related functions may offer you romantic opportunities as well. On the other hand, be careful not to mix up your workplace relationships with romantic ideals. This could complicate some of your professional activities.

Improving your luck

You'll want more money and a life of leisure and ease in 2009. Keep working on your strengths and eliminate your negative personality traits to create greater luck and harmony in your life.

Moderate all your actions and don't focus exclusively on money and material objects. Feed your spiritual needs as well. By balancing the inner and outer you'll see that your romantic and professional life will be enhanced more easily.

The 1st, 8th, 15th and 20th hours on Fridays will be very lucky for you and new opportunities will arise for you at those times. You can use the numbers 6, 15, 24 and 33 to increase luck in your general affairs.

7 = Year of Neptune

Overview

The last and most evolved sign of the zodiac is Pisces, which is ruled by Neptune. The number 7 is deeply connected with this zodiacal sign and governs you in 2009. Your ideals seem to be clearer and more spiritually orientated than ever before. Your desire to evolve and understand your inner self will be a double-edged sword. It depends on how organised you are as to how well you can use these spiritual and abstract concepts in your practical life.

Your past emotional hurts and deep emotional issues will be dealt with and removed for good, if you are serious about becoming a better human being.

Spend a little more time caring for yourself rather than others, as it's likely some of your friends will drain you of energy with their own personal problems. Of course, you mustn't turn a blind eye to the needs of others, but don't ignore your own personal needs in the process.

Love and pleasure

Meeting people with similar life views and spiritual aspirations will rekindle your faith in relationships. If you do choose to develop a new romance, make sure that there is a clear understanding of the responsibilities of one to the other. Don't get swept off your feet by people who have ulterior motives.

Keep your relationships realistic and see that the most idealistic partnerships must eventually come down to Earth. Deal with the practicalities of life.

Work

This is a year of hard work, but one in which you'll come to understand the deeper significance of your professional ideals. You may discover a whole new aspect to your career, which involves a more compassionate and self-sacrificing side to your personality.

You'll also find that your way of working will change and that you'll be more focused and able to get into the spirit of whatever you do. Finding meaningful work is very likely and therefore this could be a year when money, security, creativity and spirituality overlap to bring you a great sense of personal satisfaction.

Tapping into your greater self through meditation and self-study will bring you great benefits throughout 2009.

Improving your luck

Using self-sacrifice along with discrimination will be an unusual method of improving your luck. The laws of karma state that what you give, you receive in greater measure. This is one of the principal themes for you in 2009.

The 1st, 8th, 15th and 20th hours of Tuesdays are your lucky times. The numbers 7, 16, 25 and 34 should be used to increase your lucky energies.

8 = Year of Saturn

Overview

The earthy and practical sign of Capricorn and its ruler Saturn are intimately linked to the number 8, which rules you in 2009. Your discipline and far-sightedness will help you achieve great things in the coming year. With cautious discernment, slowly but surely you will reach your goals.

It may be that due to the influence of the solitary Saturn, your best work and achievement will be behind closed doors away from the limelight. You mustn't fear this as you'll discover many new things about yourself. You'll learn just how strong you really are.

Love and pleasure

Work will overshadow your personal affairs in 2009, but you mustn't let this erode the personal relationships you have. Becoming a workaholic brings great material successes but will also cause you to become too insular and aloof. Your family members won't take too kindly to you working 100-hour weeks.

Responsibility is one of the key words for this number and you will therefore find yourself in a position of authority that leaves very little time for fun. Try to make time to enjoy the company of friends and family and by all means schedule time off on the weekends as it will give you the peace of mind you're looking for.

Because of your responsible attitude it will be very hard for you not to assume a greater role in your workplace and this indicates longer working hours with the likelihood of a promotion with equally good remuneration.

Work

Money is high on your agenda in 2009. Number 8 is a good money number according to the Chinese and this year is at last likely to bring you the fruits of your hard labour. You are cautious and resourceful in all your dealings and will not waste your hard-earned savings. You will also be very conscious of using your time wisely.

You will be given more responsibilities and you're likely to take them on, if only to prove to yourself that you can handle whatever life dishes up.

Expect a promotion in which you will play a leading role in your work. Your diligence and hard work will pay off, literally, in a bigger salary and more respect from others.

Improving your luck

Caution is one of the key characteristics of the number 8 and is linked to Capricorn. But being overly cautious could cause you to miss valuable opportunities. If an offer is put to you, try to think outside the square and balance it with your naturally cautious nature.

Be gentle and kind to yourself. By loving yourself, others will naturally love you, too. The 1st, 8th, 15th and 20th hours of Saturdays are exceptionally lucky for you as are the numbers 1, 8, 17, 26 and 35.

9 = Year of Mars

Overview

You are now entering the final year of a nine-year cycle dominated by the planet Mars and the sign of Aries. You'll be completing many things and are determined to be successful after several years of intense work.

Some of your relationships may now have reached their use-by date and even these personal affairs may need to be released. Don't let arguments and disagreements get in the road of friendly resolution in these areas of your life.

Mars is a challenging planet and, this year, although you will be very active and productive, you may find others trying to obstruct the achievement of your goals. As a result you may react strongly to them, thereby creating disharmony in your workplace. Don't be so impulsive or reckless, and generally slow things down. The slower, steadier approach has greater merit this year.

Love and pleasure

If you become too bossy and pushy with friends this year you will just end up pushing them out of your life. It's a year to end certain friendships but by the same token it could be the perfect time to end conflicts and thereby bolster your love affairs in 2009.

If you're feeling a little irritable and angry with those you love, try getting rid of these negative feelings through some intense, rigorous sports and physical activity. This will definitely relieve tension and improve your personal life.

Work

Because you're healthy and able to work at a more intense pace you'll achieve an incredible amount in the coming year. Overwork could become a problem if you're not careful.

Because the number 9 and Mars are infused with leadership energy, you'll be asked to take the reins of the job and steer your company or group in a certain direction. This will bring with it added responsibility but also a greater sense of purpose for you.

Improving your luck

Because of the hot and restless energy of the number 9, it is important to create more mental peace in your life this year. Lower the temperature, so to speak, and decompress your relationships rather than becoming aggravated. Try to talk to your work partners and loved ones rather than telling them what to do. This will generally pick up your health and your relationships.

The 1st, 8th, 15th and 20th hours of Tuesdays are the luckiest for you this year and, if you're involved in any disputes or need to attend to health issues, these times are also very good for the best results. Your lucky numbers are 9, 18, 27 and 36.

2009:
Your Daily Planner

The most I can do for my friend is
simply be his friend

—David Henry Thoreau

There is a little-known branch of astrology called electional astrology, and it can help you select the most appropriate times for many of your day-to-day activities.

Ancient astrologers understood the planetary patterns and how they impacted on each of us. This allowed them to suggest the best possible times to start various important activities. Many farmers today still use this approach: they understand the phases of the Moon, and attest to the fact that planting seeds on certain lunar days produces a far better crop than planting on other days.

The following section covers many areas of daily life, and uses the cycles of the Moon and the combined strength of the other planets to work out the best times to start different types of activity.

So to create your own personal almanac, first select the activity you are interested in, and then quickly scan the year for the best months to start it. When you have selected the month, you can finetune your timing by finding the best specific dates. You can then be sure that the planetary energies will be in sync with you, offering you the best possible outcome.

Coupled with what you know about your monthly and weekly trends, the daily planner can be a powerful tool to help you capitalise on opportunities that come your way this year.

Good luck, and may the planets bless you with great success, fortune and happiness in 2009!

Starting activities

How many times have you made a new year's resolution to begin a diet or be a better person in your relationships? And how many times has it not worked out? Well, the reason may be partly that you started out at the wrong time! How successful you are is strongly influenced by the position of the Moon and the planets when you begin a particular activity. You could be more successful with the following activities if you start them on the days indicated.

Relationships

We all feel more empowered on some days than on others. This is because the planets have some power over us—their movement and their relationships to each other determine the ebb and flow of our energies. And our level of self-confidence and our sense of romantic magnetism play an important part in the way we behave in relationships.

Your daily planner tells you the ideal dates for meeting new friends, initiating a love affair, spending time with family and loved ones—it even tells you the most appropriate times for sexual encounters.

You'll be surprised at how much more impact you make in your relationships when you tune yourself in to the planetary energies on these special dates.

Falling in love/restoring love

During these times you could expect favourable energies to meet your soulmate or, if you've had difficulty in a relationship, to approach the one you love to rekindle both your and their emotional responses:

January	28, 30
February	25, 26
March	6, 7, 8, 28, 29, 30
April	25, 26, 30
May	1, 2, 5, 7, 26, 27, 28, 29

June	2, 3, 23, 24, 26, 29, 30
July	22, 23, 26, 27
August	14, 15, 16, 17, 22, 23, 24
September	10, 14, 16, 19, 20, 21
October	9, 10, 11, 12, 13
November	25, 26
December	22, 23, 27, 31

Special times with friends and family

Socialising, partying and having a good time with those you enjoy being with is highly favourable under the following dates. These dates are excellent to spend time with family and loved ones in a domestic environment:

January	26
February	8, 12, 13, 14, 22, 23, 24
March	8, 22, 23
April	19, 27, 28
May	1, 2, 15, 16, 17, 24, 25, 28, 29
June	2, 3, 11, 12, 13, 22, 30
July	23, 26, 27
August	5, 6, 23, 24
September	16
October	13
November	8, 10, 24
December	19, 20, 21, 29

Healing or resuming relationships

If you're trying to get back together with the one you love and need a heart-to-heart or deep and meaningful, you can try the following dates to do so:

January	5, 8, 11, 12, 18, 19, 20, 21, 22, 23, 24, 25, 26, 28, 30
February	8, 12, 13, 14
March	8
April	18, 19
May	1, 2, 28, 29
June	2, 3, 30
July	23, 26, 27
August	23, 24
September	16
October	13
November	8
December	22, 23, 27

Sexual encounters

Physical and sexual energies are well favoured on the following dates. The energies of the planets enhance your moments of intimacy during these times:

January	5, 30
February	25, 26
March	6, 7, 8, 28, 29, 30
April	25, 26, 30
May	1, 2, 5, 7, 26, 27, 28, 29

June	2, 3, 23, 24, 26, 29, 30
July	22, 23, 26, 27
August	23, 24
September	16
October	13
November	25, 26
December	22, 23, 27, 31

Health and wellbeing

Your aura and life force are susceptible to the movements of the planets; in particular, they respond to the phases of the Moon.

The following dates are the most appropriate times to begin a diet, have cosmetic surgery, or seek medical advice. They also tell you when the best times are to help others.

Feeling of wellbeing

Your physical as well as your mental alertness should be strong on these following dates. You can plan your activities and expect a good response from others:

January	8, 9, 26, 27
February	4, 5, 22, 23
March	31
April	18, 19, 27, 28
May	16, 17
June	21, 22
July	19
August	5, 6, 24, 25

September	12, 28, 30
October	8, 9
November	8, 10
December	19, 20, 21, 29, 30

Healing and medicine

This is good for approaching others who have expertise at a time when you need some deeper understanding. This is also favourable for any sort of healing or medication and making appointments with doctors or psychologists. Planning surgery around these dates should bring good results.

Often giving up our time and energy to assist others doesn't necessarily result in the expected outcome. By lending a helping hand to a friend on the following dates, the results should be favourable:

January	1, 20, 21, 22, 23, 24, 25, 26, 27, 28, 29, 30, 31
February	9, 10, 11, 12, 13, 14, 15, 16, 17, 18, 19, 20, 21, 22, 23, 24, 25, 26, 27, 28
March	2, 3, 4, 5, 6, 7, 8, 9, 22, 26, 28, 29, 30, 31
April	1, 10, 12, 15, 18, 20, 27, 28, 29, 30
May	1, 3, 7, 8, 9, 10, 11, 12
June	6, 7, 9, 13, 14, 15, 19, 21, 22
July	5, 6, 7, 8, 10, 12, 18, 19, 20, 25, 26
August	6, 7, 8, 9, 10, 29, 30, 31
September	1, 6, 27
October	8, 9, 10, 11, 12, 25, 26
November	18, 19, 20, 21, 22
December	10, 11, 12

Money

Money is an important part of life, and involves many decisions; decisions about borrowing, investing, spending. The ideal times for transactions are very much influenced by the planets, and whether your investment or nest egg grows or doesn't grow can often be linked to timing. Making your decisions on the following dates could give you a whole new perspective on your financial future.

Managing wealth and money

To build your nest egg, it's a good time to open your bank account and invest money on the following dates:

January	3, 4, 5, 10, 11, 16, 17, 23, 24, 25, 31
February	1, 6, 7, 12, 13, 14, 20, 21, 27, 28
March	5, 6, 7, 12, 13, 19, 26, 27
April	2, 3, 8, 9, 15, 17, 23, 24, 29, 30
May	5, 6, 7, 13, 14, 20, 21, 26, 27
June	2, 3, 9, 10, 16, 17, 18, 23, 24, 29, 30
July	6, 7, 8, 14, 15, 20, 21, 26, 27
August	2, 3, 4, 10, 11, 17, 18, 23, 24, 30, 31
September	6, 7, 13, 14, 19, 20, 26, 27
October	3, 4, 5, 10, 11, 16, 17, 18, 23, 24, 25, 31
November	1, 6, 7, 13, 14, 20, 21, 27, 28
December	4, 5, 10, 11, 17, 18, 24, 25, 26, 31

Spending

It's always fun to spend but the following dates are more in tune with this activity and are likely to give you better results:

January	20, 28, 30
February	3
March	28, 29, 30
April	25, 26
May	31
June	1, 2, 7, 8, 9, 10, 28, 30
July	1, 2, 3, 26, 27, 29, 30
August	2, 3, 4, 5, 20, 21, 22, 23, 24, 25
September	19, 20, 21, 22, 23
October	9, 10
November	1, 7, 8, 17
December	27, 28

Selling

If you're thinking of selling something, whether it is small or large, consider the following dates as ideal times to do so:

January	3, 18, 19, 20, 21, 25, 26, 27, 28, 29, 30, 31
February	8, 10, 11, 12, 13, 14, 15, 18, 20, 22, 23, 24, 26, 28
March	2, 3, 4, 5, 6, 7, 8, 9, 16, 26, 27, 28, 31
April	5, 10, 19, 20, 23, 25, 27, 28, 29
May	1, 2, 7, 9, 13, 14, 21, 24, 25, 28, 29, 31
June	1, 2, 7, 8, 14, 16, 17, 20, 21, 22, 26, 30
July	1, 2, 3, 9, 10, 11, 15, 16, 17, 26, 27
August	2, 3, 4, 13, 14, 15, 16, 17
September	1, 2, 3, 4, 5, 6, 14, 15, 16, 17, 21, 22, 23, 24, 25, 26, 27, 28, 30, 31

October	1, 2, 3, 4, 5, 6, 7, 8, 9, 10, 11, 12, 31
November	2, 3, 9, 10, 11, 12, 13, 25, 26, 27, 28, 29, 30
December	1, 2, 3, 7, 8, 9, 17, 20

Borrowing

Few of us like to borrow money, but if you must, taking out a loan on the following dates should be positive:

January	11, 18, 19, 20, 23, 24, 25
February	15, 16, 20, 21
March	14, 15, 19, 20
April	10, 11, 12, 15, 16, 17
May	9, 13, 14
June	9, 10
July	7, 8, 20, 21
August	17, 18
September	13, 14
October	10, 11
November	6, 7, 15, 16
December	4, 5, 12, 13, 14

Work and education

Your career is important to you, and continual improvement of your skills is therefore also crucial, professionally, mentally and socially. The dates below will help you find out the most appropriate times to improve your professional talents and commence new work or education associated with your work.

You may need to decide when to start learning a new skill, when to ask for a promotion, and even when to make an important career change. Here are the days when mental and educational power is strong.

Learning new skills

Educational pursuits are lucky and bring good results on the following dates:

January	8, 9
February	4, 5
March	3, 4, 10, 31
April	1, 6, 7, 27, 28
May	3, 4, 25, 30, 31
June	1, 6, 7, 27, 28
July	4, 5, 24, 25, 31
August	1, 21, 22, 27, 28, 29
September	23, 24, 25
October	21, 22
November	17, 18, 19
December	29, 30

Changing career path or profession

If you're feeling stuck and need to move into a new professional activity, changing jobs can be done at these times:

January	6, 7
February	2, 3
March	1, 2, 3, 4, 5, 6, 7, 8, 9, 10, 28, 29, 30
April	6, 7, 25, 26
May	3, 4, 30, 31
June	1, 27, 28

July	6, 24, 25
August	2, 3, 4, 21, 22, 30, 31
September	26, 27
October	23, 24, 25
November	2, 20, 21, 29, 30
December	1, 17, 18, 27, 28

Promotion, professional focus and hard work

To increase your mental focus and achieve good results from the work you do, promotions are likely on these dates that follow:

January	4, 5, 6, 11, 12, 13, 14, 15, 16, 21
February	6
March	18, 19, 20
April	8, 28, 29
May	12, 21
June	25, 26
July	1, 2, 3, 8, 15, 17
August	4, 14, 15, 16, 17, 18, 22, 23, 24
September	14, 15, 18, 19, 23, 24, 25, 26
October	22
November	7, 10, 11, 12, 17
December	1, 2, 3, 7, 28

Travel

Setting out on a holiday or adventurous journey is exciting. To gain the most out of your holidays and journeys, travelling on the following dates is likely to give you a sense of fulfilment:

January	9, 10, 28, 29, 30, 31
February	1, 4, 5, 26
March	3, 4, 5, 6, 7, 27, 31
April	27, 28, 29
May	1, 2, 25
June	6, 7, 25, 26
July	6, 31
August	1, 2, 21, 22, 23, 24, 29
September	19, 20, 23, 24, 25, 26, 27
October	1, 2, 3, 25, 28, 29, 30, 31
November	1, 17, 18, 26, 28
December	17, 18, 23, 26

Beauty and grooming

Believe it or not, cutting your hair or nails has a powerful effect on your body's electromagnetic energy. If you cut your hair or nails at the wrong time of the month, you can reduce your level of vitality significantly. Use these dates to ensure you optimise your energy levels by staying in tune with the stars.

Hair and nails

January	1, 2, 8, 9, 21, 22, 28, 29, 30
February	4, 5, 17, 18, 19, 25, 26
March	3, 4, 16, 17, 18, 24, 25, 31
April	1, 13, 14, 20, 21, 22, 27, 28, 29, 30
May	8, 10, 11, 12, 18, 19, 24, 25
June	6, 7, 8, 14, 15, 21, 22

July	4, 5, 11, 12, 13, 18, 19, 31
August	1, 7, 8, 9, 14, 15, 16, 27, 28, 29
September	4, 5, 11, 12, 23, 24, 25
October	1, 2, 8, 9, 21, 22, 28, 29, 30
November	4, 5, 17, 18, 19, 25, 26
December	2, 3, 15, 16, 22, 23, 29, 30

Therapies, massage and self-pampering

January	18, 19, 20, 26, 27
February	3, 6, 7, 8, 12, 13, 14, 15, 16, 22, 23, 24
March	6, 8, 28, 29, 30
April	5, 8, 9, 18, 19, 25, 26, 29, 30
May	1, 2, 5, 7, 9, 15, 16, 17, 22, 23, 26, 27, 28, 29
June	2, 3, 4, 5, 11, 12, 13, 19, 20, 23, 24, 26, 30
July	1, 2, 3, 9, 10, 23, 26, 27, 28, 29, 30
August	6, 12, 13, 17, 18, 19, 20, 23, 24, 25, 26
September	1, 2, 13, 14, 16
October	10, 11, 12, 13, 16, 17, 27
November	8, 9, 10, 13, 16, 23, 24, 29, 30
December	1, 4, 5, 6, 7, 10, 11, 12, 13, 14, 19, 20, 21, 27, 28, 31

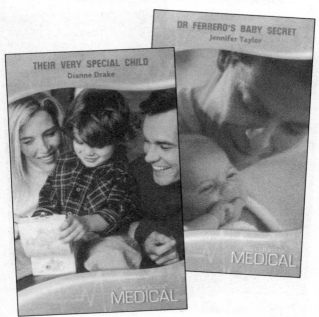

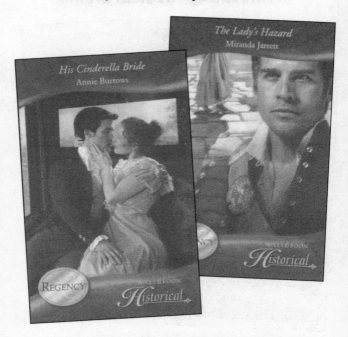

Life, love and family

6 brand-new titles each month

Available on the third Friday of every month
from WHSmith, ASDA, Tesco
and all good bookshops
www.millsandboon.co.uk

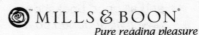